Complete Camping Handbook

Everything You Need to Know – Before You Go

This book is dedicated to our awesome children, Michael and Emma. Thanks for being who you are, the joy you've brought to our lives, and all the wonderful memories. Happy Camping guys!

Complete Camping Handbook, Everything You Need to Know – Before You Go by David Zinck

Table of Contents

Introduction

"Keep close to Nature's heart…and break clear away, once in a while, and climb a mountain or spend a week in the woods. Wash your spirit clean." (John Muir)

My wife and I have been camping together for over 40 years. We want you to enjoy camping and the Great Outdoors as much as we have – and still do!

To help you get the most out of your camping adventures, we've put together this camping handbook built on our experiences – and misfortunes – and through our research on camping equipment.

Many people have terrible first-camping experiences and never go again. *Don't be one of those people*! We want to help make your camping trips wonderful experiences so you'll continue to reap the benefits of the Great Outdoors and pass on these pleasures to your children and friends.

We started out with a small pup tent, just big enough for the two of us – it was so small, you couldn't even sit up inside. We picked fruit one summer in the Okanagan Valley in British Columbia, Canada and lived almost all summer in that tent - somehow. Thinking back on it now, I really don't know how we did it…

We eventually moved up to a 4-man tent – wow, we were impressed! – and on to a large cabin tent big enough for a family of four and our two dogs.

After using tents for almost 40 years, we decided to do some glamping and bought a small camper van – I guess we're getting old? Ha! We still spend most of our time outside the camper, but packing up is so much easier.

We love camping – exploring new areas, the smell of a campfire, lots of fresh air and exercise, eating food cooked over a fire, spending time with family and friends – there are so many benefits to camping and appreciating the simple things in life that nature has to offer.

Camping is healthy, enjoyable, and super relaxing – in all kinds of weather. When it rains, we get our umbrellas out and set up a tarp. If it's cold we take extra blankets and clothing.

We've camped on beaches by the ocean, set up our tents next to lakes and rivers, enjoyed camping in the forest, and hiked the famous West Coast Trail in British Columbia.

What do you get in this book? We've put together a guide to help you, whether you're a total beginner or a more experienced camper.

This is not a guide for RVers, although there is lots of info that will benefit RVers too. It's aimed mainly at car and tent campers. The equipment-buying guides will be of help to backpackers as well.

You'll find 15 chapters full of camping information to help you make the most of your experiences.

- You'll learn camping basics, such as what to pack, how to set up a tarp to stay dry, how to cook over a campfire, how to tie a few basic knots, where to camp, and much more.

- The equipment guide chapters will help you decide what camping equipment is right for you, including tents, sleeping bags, flashlights, camp stoves, and sleeping mattresses and pads.

- We've included a chapter on cooking outdoors too. Everyone knows how to cook hotdogs and make smores – we'll tell you how we make

Thanksgiving turkey dinner over the campfire, smoke the fish we catch, and we've included recipes for egg muffins, pizza, bread, and even desserts.

- The chapters on camping with children and pets incorporate our experiences and misfortunes with cats and dogs, and the totally enjoyable outdoor experiences we've had with our children.

- We've camped in places without showers and toilets, so you'll find a chapter on nature's toiletry, including instructions for making your own portable toilet and shower.

- You'll learn how to build a campfire using natural tinder and how to make your own fire-starter.

- Predatory animals exist in almost every natural space. Learn what to do if you meet a bear or cougar on your travels.

Enjoy camping and the outdoors!

Chapter 1: Where to Camp

"Without the intense touch of nature, you can never fully freshen yourself! Go for a camping and there both your weary mind and your exhausted body will rise like a morning sun!" (Mehmet Murat ildan)

So you've decided to go camping – maybe for the first time ever. But where do you go? Do you want a swimming pool or a beach? Lakeside or oceanfront?

Do you need showers? Internet? Flush toilets? Running water? Electricity?

We've camped in public and government sites, on the beach, and in remote places with no facilities and enjoyed all of our experiences – although we have had a few bumps along the way.

You have to decide on your priorities before you leave your house. Some things to consider are:

- **Availability:** Make sure there are sites available in the campground you choose. You might consider reserving a site in popular parks – some charge reservation fees, and many offer online reservations. Some campgrounds operate strictly on a first come, first served basis. Weekends are the busiest time, so maybe camping through the week will provide more availability options.

- **Privacy:** Do you want to be alone or close to other campers? Will you feel comfortable or isolated in remote campgrounds? Especially after dark…

- **Noise:** Can you tolerate a noisy campground, or do you want absolute quiet and solitude? Do you have children who would like others to play with, or do you want a campground without the noise of kids having fun? Many campers are inconsiderate and party all night or operate a generator early in the morning and late at night.

- **Amenities:** Do you need hot showers? Flush toilets or pit toilets? Swimming pool and playground? Internet, electricity, and running water? Fire pits and available firewood? Laundry?

- **Activities:** Potluck dinners with other campers, hiking and biking trails, games such as horseshoes or badminton, fishing, guided nature interpretive tours. Many places have campground hosts to help you find local activities and attractions.

- **Type of campground:** RV only with hookups, RVs and tents, tents only, walk-in or drive-in sites, free sites, wilderness sites.

- **Wildlife:** Be sure to research your chosen camping area for warnings of bears, cougars, and other animals that may decide to eat you, your children, or your pets. Refer to **Chapter 10: "Bears, Cougars, and Other Dangerous Stuff"** for more info.

Private campgrounds are unpredictable. Choose carefully. Most are very well kept and quiet while others can be a dirty and noisy nightmare.

Some are awesome with lots of trees for shade, private sites, clean bathrooms, swimming pools, electric and sewer hookups for RVs, internet connections, and enforced quiet times.

Others are basically big fields with no trees, no privacy between sites, noisy generators running constantly, noisy people everywhere, overflowing garbage cans, and filthy facilities.

Government campgrounds, in our experience, are more predictable. You can normally expect to find clean, well-run campgrounds with enforced regulations.

Most have private sites, some with hook-ups for RVs, and most have walk-in sites for tent campers wanting more privacy and quiet. Some offer backcountry campsites that you can access by hiking or canoeing.

The campground you choose can make the difference between a wonderful experience and a total nightmare.

Research the campsite before your stay. The internet provides the means to check out a campsite before you choose where to go. We've included a list of review websites covering North America.

Some of these sites are dedicated to RVs, but many RV campgrounds have tenting sites available as well.

Note: Check the date of the review. Many reviews are outdated with inaccurate pricing, etc. Read the reviews with current dates.

Campground review websites:

- https://www.tripadvisor.com/ (Worldwide)
- http://www.rvparkreviews.com/ (US, Canada, Mexico)
- https://www.campendium.com/ (US and Canada)
- https://www.goodsam.com/campgrounds-rv-parks/reviews/ (US and Canada)
- http://www.camping-canada.com/ (Canada only)
- https://thedyrt.com/camping (US only)
- https://www.rvbuddy.com/ (US only)

Government campgrounds

Federal, provincial, and state government websites have listings of campgrounds available in all geographic locations in North America. Information and brochures are often available at local tourist offices.

Free campsites

You can find free camping areas in almost every area of North America. Most of these sites have few, if any, amenities. Some have designated camping sites, picnic tables, fire pits, and vault toilets. Many are totally unsupervised, but most people using them are respectful of others and their surroundings.

"Free Campsites" is a great website resource to find free camping areas in your region: https://freecampsites.net/ Just start typing the free-camping location you want in the search box and choose from one of the locations in the dropdown. A list and map of free campsites in that area will appear.

In Canada, free camping is available on some Crown lands. You'll need to check each provincial website for more information and regulations.

Other campground resources

We've found a few websites you can check out for more camping locations.

British Columbia offers camping in provincial recreation sites. Some are free, some charge a small fee. Some are remote, some close to civilization. You can check out the camping sites and trails here: http://www.sitesandtrailsbc.ca/

Some Forest Service land in the US is available for camping. You can check out their website here: https://www.fs.fed.us/visit/destinations

Visit the US National Forest Campground Guide's website to find a camping spot in your area: https://www.forestcamping.com/dow/list/nflist.htm

Choose your camping area carefully, and decide exactly what you need for amenities before you go. We choose solitude, scenery, and hiking trails over RV campsites. Our children were happy with natural attractions and nature rather than swimming pools and playgrounds.

Chapter 2: Camping Equipment

"Camping is nature's way of promoting the motel business." (Dave Barry)

You gotta love Dave Barry's humour, but camping is one of our favourite activities, and we've gathered a lot of camping equipment and experience over the years.

Make a list! Check it at least twice. We've been using a checklist for many years. It makes packing up so much easier and faster and we don't forget things. It can be aggravating to drive for hours to a beautiful, secluded campsite only to discover that you forgot sleeping bags – or worse – your tent.

We print off copies of our continually-updated list and simply check off everything on the list until we were ready to roll.

Following is a (long) inventory of all the things you could take with you to make your camping trip comfortable and fun. If you're going backpacking to a wilderness site, you absolutely will not be able to take all the things listed below – you'll have to make do with a small tent and few less "glamping" items…

Go through all the following gear and decide what you'll take and make your own list, update as necessary, and print a checklist before you go.

Basic Camping Gear

Tent

Obviously, you need a tent – or some type of shelter – whether it's a lean-to, a pup tent, or a tent big enough for the whole family. There is a wide range of tents from which to choose. Refer to **Chapter 12: "How to Choose a Tent"** to help you pick one that's right for you.

Tent designs include the basic ridge tent (no standing up in these), cabin tents, various-sized dome and geodesic tents, quick-pitch tents, large family tents – even inflatable models.

On the other hand, maybe you are a hammock camper who likes to hang out in the trees. Some people like to sleep out in the open or under a lean-to, while others need a fully equipped RV.

Make sure the tent you pick is large enough for all the people who will be sleeping in it. If you have children and/or pets, you'll need twice as much room as you think! Even more important, make certain that it's waterproof and durable.

Another consideration is wind – we've had wet tents blow down on top of us in the middle of the night a few times – in the pouring rain. Pegging your tent down securely is a must! You should have extra pegs and lots of tie-down line. By placing your tent close to trees, you will be able to secure some of your tie-downs to trunks and branches.

Tarp

A tarp is crucial for keeping the rain off the campsite – and it seems to rain at least once during every camping trip. It will also shield you from the hot rays of the sun, and can serve as a windbreak for those breezy areas along the lake or seashore.

We have a tarp that's big enough to cover our tent and a good portion of the campsite, including the fire pit, so we can enjoy a campfire even on rainy nights.

If your tarp is set up properly, you'll be able to cook, sit outside, and enjoy a campfire – all in the pouring rain – and all the campers without tarps will be green with envy as they sit huddled in their tents and cars.

Read **Chapter 3: "Tarp Setup (Keeping Your Campsite and Campfire Dry)"** for more information.

Axe or Hatchet, Saw, Knife, and Fire-starter

If you plan to have a fire – and what's camping without one – you'll need a good **short-handled axe or hatchet** to split your firewood into easy-to-light kindling. Make sure it's sharp and the head is fastened securely. You can use it to drive your tent pegs into the ground too, so you don't need to bring along a hammer.

*HINT: Make the wooden handle of the axe swell and fit tightly into the head by soaking it in water – so it doesn't fly off into someone's tent while you're hacking up your firewood.

A good sharp saw will allow you to cut up sticks and branches around your campsite easily, rather than trying to break them. A saw with a folding blade is the best idea, so that the teeth are protected to keep them sharp, and so that you don't cut yourself when digging around the trunk of your car or under the seat trying to find the saw that you know you packed because you checked it off on the camp list before you left home.

A sharp pocketknife will come in handy for cutting your tarp and tie-down ropes and lines, and you'll probably want to cut hot dog and marshmallow sticks too. My favourite type of knife is a small, lightweight, folding pocketknife with a locking blade – the locked blade won't fold in on your fingers while in use.

Buy some type of sharpening device – a whetstone, sharpening steel, or knife sharpener. You're more likely to cut yourself with a dull knife than with a sharp one – dull knives have a tendency to slip rather than bite into whatever you're trying to cut.

We make sure we have lots of old newspapers for starting the kindling. If you forget, Old Man's Beard is an excellent replacement. It's a greenish lichen that loves to grow on old fir and spruce trees. Look for dead branches with green, hairy stuff growing on them and break off small pieces – it'll ignite quickly, and will burn even in the rain.

Read **Chapter 4: "How to Build A Campfire"** for more info on fire starter and how to make your own.

Sleeping Bags, Pads and Pillows

Getting a good sleep could be the most important factor in enjoying your camping trip.

You'll want to be comfortable and warm in your tent, so you'll need a good sleeping bag, and for extra comfort, an air mattress or sleeping pad, and pillows. If you have extra room, pack a blanket or two as well for unexpected, extra-cold nights.

For more information on air mattresses and sleeping bags, refer to **Chapter 13: "How to Choose an Air Mattress, Sleeping Pad, or Bed"** and **Chapter 14: "How to Choose a Sleeping Bag"**.

The basic square sleeping bag gives you room to move your feet and can be zipped together with another square bag so you can snuggle up with your partner.

Mummy bags are tapered toward the bottom to help keep warm air inside and close to your body – some are designed for use in sub-zero temperatures. However, you can't zip these together for snuggling – what fun is that?

You can get sleeping bags that let you move freely. These are called sleeping pods or barrel-shaped bags and are ideal for people who toss and turn in their sleep. They are half as wide as they are long providing lots of legroom.

Sleeping bags have different temperature ratings, so you can choose whatever grade you think you'll need. You can also choose right or left-hand zippers, children's bags, double-size, different types of insulations, whether or not you want a hood, a pocket, or a pillow. There are so many choices!

Mattresses and pads come in several forms: air mattresses (some self-inflatable), foam ground pads, and bubble pads. Some people use thick foam slabs, which are comfortable and warm, but very bulky.

The self-inflatables take up less room, you don't need a pump, you can buy them in different sizes, and they come with different R -values (insulation thickness) for warmth.

Sleeping cots are popular as well – an air mattress or pad with legs. We upgraded to an inflatable bed on a stand after many years of sleeping on the ground – a real treat!

If you have a blow-up air mattress, don't forget the pump! We've taken turns blowing them up with lung power more than once… You can buy hand-powered or battery operated pumps – some plug into a power outlet in your vehicle.

*HINT: If you buy a sturdy air mattress, you can use it at the beach or lake to float on.

Comfortable pillows are important to us for a good night's sleep. We've slept without pillows or used bundled-up clothing but nothing beats your favourite head rest. If you have the extra space, put pillows on your checklist.

Inflatable models are a space-saving option if you can find a really comfortable model. A happy, restful sleep can make a big difference in how you enjoy the next day. You don't want to wake up feeling cranky – or worse – having a cranky morning partner. Walking around with a stiff neck all day takes away from the camping experience for sure.

Go for maximum comfort. Invest in good sleeping equipment. It could make the difference between a one-and-only camping trip and a lifetime of rewarding experiences.

Coolers and Water Containers

You can choose from hard or soft coolers, coolers on wheels, or electric coolers that plug into a power outlet in your vehicle; some have straps for carrying on your back, others are collapsible…just make sure the one you buy has plenty of room. We have two coolers – one for food, one for drinks.

Whatever cooler you pick, make certain it will keep things cold! It's worth the extra cost to have a good, well-insulated cooler. There's nothing more disappointing than putting ice in your cooler and a couple of hours later you find that it has melted. We like our beer cold and expect the cooler to do its job all day and night!

Choose a cooler that seals securely. We woke up one morning to find all of our food strewn across a hillside in Fundy National Park, New Brunswick. Raccoons figured out how to open the cover clamps. They even drank our milk! They didn't get our beer though – I guess it was too hard for them to open…

Tips:

- Blocks of ice last much longer than cubes. Fill a few containers, leaving a bit of room for expansion, and freeze them a few days before your trip to ensure they are frozen solid. You can use containers such as clean soda bottles and milk cartons. You can drink the water as it melts too.

- Freeze most of your perishable foods – the stuff that can be frozen, such as meats and fish. Similar to an ice block, it will thaw slowly – take the food out as you need it to thaw quickly.

- Make sure everything you plan to put into the cooler is cold – put everything in your refrigerator overnight.

- Chill your cooler before packing. Fill it with ice-cold water or ice to cool it down as much as possible.

- Put your ice cubes for drinks in a separate container for easy access and to keep them clean.

- Common sense dictates that you make sure your cooler is in the shade, not in a hot car trunk or direct sunlight. If you go for a long hike, make sure it will be in the shade while you're gone.

You will use a lot more water than you think! We carry, at minimum, a 20-litre (5-gallon) water jug with us – you can't always get fresh drinking water where you camp. Make sure your container is big enough to keep you supplied, especially if there is no drinkable water on site.

Collapsible water bags are great for filling at the campsite where potable water is available and take up very little room when packing.

We also bring small, insulated water bottles for hiking.

Purify water from a lake or stream before drinking – it may contain harmful contaminants. You could boil it for about 10 minutes but this uses fuel. Chemical treatment is another option, or you could use filters and purifiers, including UV light purifiers.

Many purifying options are available from outdoor supply stores. Talk to sales staff to choose the system that's right for your needs. You can choose a large purification system with a water dispenser, a small unit for backpacking, or something in between.

Camp Stove, Grill, and Coffee Pot

A propane, butane, or naphtha gas camp stove is great for fast cooking. We've always used stoves with two burners. We've owned both naphtha gas and propane models.

Please refer to **Chapter 15: "How to Choose a Camp Stove"** for more info.

A grill is a must-have item for us. We do a lot of cooking over the campfire. We've recycled old BBQ grills and oven racks, but you could purchase one made from stainless steel or even have one custom made. You'll also need a good brush or pad for cleaning it – one of our dogs used to clean ours up pretty good if we didn't keep an eye on him.

A good coffee pot is a necessity for us. The first thing we do in the morning is light the camp stove, put the coffee pot on, and light a fire! We have a 10-cup, stainless steel percolator – we couldn't go camping without it.

Alternately, you could use a French press. They are available in stainless steel camping models.

Single-cup coffee filters work well and, if you forgot to put the coffee maker on your list, you could try paper towels or toilet paper as a filter substitute.

If you have none of these items, just dump your coffee into a cup full of hot water, stir, and let it settle for a while…

Nothing compares to sitting by a campfire, enjoying a cup of freshly perked coffee…watching the sun rise over a lake or the ocean…I wish I was camping right now...

Lanterns, Flashlights, and Headlamps

You'll need a lantern if you like lots of light in your campsite after the sun goes down. A lantern will also light up your tent so everyone can read a book or play a game before sleeping.

You need to decide exactly what you need from a lantern before you go out and buy one. Are you going to use the lamp for car-camping or backpacking? Does it need to be compact and lightweight? Some are small enough to put in your jacket pocket.

There are several options for fuel. You can choose from propane, butane, naphtha-gas, battery-operated, and rechargeable models.

*WARNING: If you plan to use a gas lantern in an enclosed area such as your tent, don't become a victim of carbon monoxide poisoning. Ensure that you have enough ventilation!

Do you have lots of room for a large, heavy, gas-powered model and the fuel to run it? Or maybe you prefer a lantern that burns no fuel, runs on batteries, is rechargeable, or is solar powered. Carrying a small solar panel rather than extra fuel on a hiking trip may make more sense.

Several models can be used as either a flashlight or a lantern, and most lanterns can double as an emergency light in your home if the power goes out.

A sturdy base is another feature to look for. You don't want your lantern to tip over – especially a hot, gas-powered unit with a glass globe.

Gas-powered lanterns can become extremely hot, so may not be suitable for use in tents and especially around children.

Price can also be a factor, with costs ranging from under $25 to well over $100 – plus the cost of any fuel, mantles, or batteries.

Large gas lanterns are generally brighter than most battery operated models but can be quite noisy at full brightness.

You need to buy fuel and mantles for gas-powered models, batteries for others, but the rechargeable models with built-in battery packs require nothing but an occasional charge.

If you already have a gas-powered camp stove – and you've decided on a gas lantern – you may want to purchase a lantern that uses the same fuel – you won't have to carry two different types of fuel on your trip.

Piezoelectric ignition might be an option to consider for gas-powered models. You just push a button for ignition instead of using matches or a lighter.

Many lanterns come with a carry case – very handy when packing fragile units with glass globes.

How bright do you need your lantern to be? Do you need to light up the entire campsite or just inside your tent? Will you need a lamp for cooking? We seldom use our bright lantern – we prefer sitting around the campfire in the near darkness, but it does come in handy for cooking when we arrive back at the campsite after dark.

Look for the lumen ratings for brightness comparisons – but don't be fooled by false advertising. For a better understanding of lumen ratings, along with water resistance, and other relevant lighting information, read the section on lumens **Chapter 11: "How to Choose a Flashlight"**.

Adjustable brightness is another factor to consider before making your purchase – most models include this feature, but check it out. You can even control some lanterns with an app on your smartphone. Some actually have a "party mode" which can sync music with a flashing mode on the lamp – party on good campers!

Certain models offer a choice of 360-degree coverage for central lighting, or 180 degrees when light is needed in only one area, and to save power.

Cost of fuel may be a deciding factor – propane and butane can be expensive, while solar or rechargeable units run for free. Crank charging is also available on some models.

For battery-powered, rechargeable, and solar-powered units, check out the run time at all brightness levels – paying more for a lantern that lasts longer may be worth it. Models with extra-long run times at low levels can be used as night-lights.

Maybe you need a USB port to charge your phone – some lanterns have this feature as well.

Another important feature to look for in a lantern is hangability – I don't think that's a word but I'm using it anyway. Look for a model that can be hung from a tree branch, a rope strung between two trees, a metal hanging bracket, a loop inside your tent – whatever's handy.

Also, consider toughness and shock-resistance. The glass globes on some models will shatter easily if dropped, while tough plastic units are much more shock resistant. Globe replacements are available for purchase for most lanterns if you do happen to break yours.

Do you need a waterproof lantern? Some models are 100% waterproof and can be submerged in water – some will even float if dropped in the lake.

A few lanterns are magnetic, so can be stuck onto a metal surface such as your vehicle.

Inflatable models are available for people who don't have a lot of extra space, such as backpackers.

Make sure you bring extra batteries, or fuel and lantern mantles for the gas-powered models – moths love to get inside the glass dome and destroy the delicate mantle, so stock up on them.

Pack lots of candles in case you run out of fuel and your flashlight batteries die – or for a romantic evening… Citronella candles will help keep the bugs at bay.

You'll also need a flashlight or headlamp for walks around the campground in the dark, for in the tent at night, and you'll definitely need one for that late-night trip to the outhouse!

Check out **Chapter 11: "How to Choose a Flashlight"** for more information on brightness and lumens, waterproof ratings, etc.

Solar lights come in handy too. We strategically place a few small ones around the campsite – close to tent doors, lighting the way to the "bathroom" facilities, and at the campsite entrance. They last most of the night on full charge and light up automatically as it gets dark.

We have a candle-powered LED light that we use all the time – it's great. Using thermoelectric technology,

one small tea light candle will run the light for hours –
we seldom use more than one candle per night. It's not
super-bright, but gives off enough light to eat by or play
backgammon and cards, and the light tilts and
telescopes up and down.

Our choice of lighting? Fuel and batteries are
expensive and result in more items to pack –
rechargeable/solar products get the nod.

We pack good quality, very bright, rechargeable
flashlights and headlamps for each of us for late night
walks – and unavoidable trips to use the "facilities". A
lamp powered by one tea-light candle, a bright,
rechargeable lantern, lots of candles – the campfire, the
stars and the full moon…

Miscellaneous Camping Equipment

- Don't forget a first aid kit!

- Pots, pans, utensils, cups, etc.

- Towels and facecloths

- Cast iron frying pan, Dutch oven, and pie iron

- You'll need a wash line, so take lots of rope or
  heavy twine and learn a few knots that you can
  untie easily. Please! Do not cut your line and
  leave unsightly pieces hanging in the trees! We
  see this all the time – be thoughtful of the next
  people to use your site.

- Bathroom supplies – soap, toothpaste,
  toothbrushes, toilet paper, etc.

- A big container or two to store all your stuff –
  make sure it's waterproof.

- A container to wash your dishes

- A few extra clothes – camping can be dirty,
  especially if you have fun hiking and having a

fire. Children have the most fun when they get dirty!

- A shovel if you go wilderness camping with no outhouse or bathroom facilities. Read **Chapter 8: "Roughing It (Primitive Toilets and Showers)"** for more info.

- Bug repellent! Lots of bug repellent and citronella candles.

- Sunscreen

- A patch kit for your inflatable air mattress

- A small broom or whisk to clean the tent

- Tongs and foil for cooking over the campfire

- Bear spray, bear bangers, bear bells, whistles, air horns, etc. if you are camping in bear, coyote, or cougar country. Make sure to hang your food high in a tree or put it inside your vehicle – never in your tent! For more info, refer to **Chapter 10: "Bears, Cougars, and Other Dangerous Stuff"**.

Notes on cast iron pots, pans, and pie irons. We've found the easiest way to clean cast iron, especially if food is burnt and seemingly welded to the pan, is to fill it with water and simmer for a while. This loosens the grime effortlessly. Clean the pan thoroughly and coat it with cooking oil to ready it for the next usage.

Optional Camping Gear

Folding camp chairs, hammock, folding table, tablecloth, small cutting board, extra blankets, rain gear, umbrellas, extra clothes, hiking boots, cards and board games, fishing gear, bikes, canoe or kayaks, duct tape, air mattress/tent repair kit, etc., etc.

Lots of food. Camping can give you a hearty appetite, so bring extra food and healthy snacks.

If you have children, you need something to keep them occupied at the campsite – other than video games. Our kids were happy with simple things – you'll find more info in **Chapter 6: "Fun Family Camping"**.

You may need a truck and trailer if you buy all the camping equipment on this list, but whatever kind of camping trip you go on – one night, a weekend, or a week-long excursion, do as the Boy Scouts do and "be prepared"!

Chapter 3: Tarp Setup (Keeping Your Campsite and Campfire Dry)

"The best thing one can do when it's raining is to let it rain." (Henry Wadsworth Longfellow)

The first thing we do when we get to our campsite – besides getting the lawn chairs out, having a beer, and relaxing for a while – is to set up our camping tarp.

You'll need a camp tarp to keep the rain off your campsite, gear, and campfire. A tarp is also great for shade on a very hot day, and we have set up tarps as wind barriers when camping by the ocean or a lake.

After having tarps that were always too small, we finally bought a large one that measures 20 feet x 30 feet – enough to keep everything in the campsite dry, including the fire. We'll show you the way we've found best to set up our tarp.

Steps to setting up your camping tarp using the ridgeline method

You should have a main support rope, or ridgeline, to hold up the tarp. Tying the rope up high and stretching it between two trees works great. Check out all the trees surrounding your campsite and decide which two you are going to use for the main support line.

The trees should align so that your ridgeline crosses the middle of your site – or as close as possible. If there are no trees in your campsite, move to another site or use poles as described below.

Make sure the tarp will cover the fire pit, and the trees are big enough to elevate the tarp sufficiently so it doesn't melt or catch on fire. If you can move your fire pit, great, but most times the fire pit cannot be moved, so pick your trees accordingly.

You'll need plenty of good, sturdy rope for the main line. You should have at least 30 metres/100 feet (you always need more than you think), with a thickness of 3/8" – 1/2".

Tie one rope end around a piece of firewood (or a rock) and throw it up into one of the trees you picked out. Get it up as high as you can. The trick is getting the piece of wood to arc over a branch or crotch in the tree, and drop down to where you can reach it.

After trying this unsuccessfully for 10 or 20 times, take a break, have another beer – or try climbing the tree. Getting the rope where you want it and high enough is usually the hardest part…

Learn to tie a few knots! When it's time to take the tarp down, you don't want to cut the rope. Not only is this a waste of good rope, but seeing rope and string hanging around campsites is unsightly – we're always cleaning up after other people. To learn how to tie a few knots, refer to **Chapter 9: "Learn How to Tie a Few Basic Knots"**.

After you get the rope looped over the tree branch, untie the piece of wood or rock, wrap the rope around the tree's trunk a few times, and tie it off with a knot that is easy to untie – you'll need to adjust it later. Some good knot choices are: bowline, clove-hitch, half-hitch, or reverse half-hitch.

Lay your rope across the ground, stretching it over to the other tree you've chosen. This will be your ridgeline. Spread your tarp over the ridgeline so that it is roughly centered. You can run the rope through the middle grommets to make it stay centered, but this usually makes setup more difficult, and it's harder to adjust the tarp later.

Repeat throwing the firewood (or rock), tied to the loose end of the rope, up into the second tree and tie it off.

Having another break is OK at this point – and, since you're camping, another beer is acceptable.

Pull the rope tight until you have the tarp at the desired height. It should be looking good by now – well above the fire pit and high enough to walk underneath from end to end. Tie the rope off in the same way you did with the other tree.

You'll need smaller, shorter ropes for securing the sides of the tarp – six or more pieces of various lengths. Attach a piece of rope to all four corners of the tarp and the grommets on each side – a bowline is a good knot here.

For windy days and added stability on the corners – so that the tarp doesn't tear – you can enclose a rock (or golf ball) in each corner of the tarp and tie the rope around the enclosed rock.

This is a useful tip to use when the corner grommets are worn or ripped out of your tarp. Tie off the corners and the sides to the nearest trees. Try to position the ropes high enough so that you don't run into them, especially in the dark.

After the tarp is up and the corners are pulled out, you can adjust it to whatever position, pitch, and angle that suits your purpose by varying the length and tension of the ropes.

If you are using the tarp for shade or wind, you may want a long, steep pitch on one side. If it's for rain, make sure both sides of the tarp slope so the rain will run off. You don't want the rain to pool inside the tarp, so make sure the lines are fairly taught and you have a nice sloping pitch.

*Hint: You can adjust the position of the tarp by sliding it back and forth along the ridgeline. When you don't want it over your campsite – you want to enjoy the sunshine and the weather is looking good – simply untie the stays at one end and slide the tarp back out of the way. If it starts to rain, you can easily slide it back over your campsite.

An alternative ridgeline tarp setup entails hanging the tarp diagonally across the main line. You need to position the tarp on the ridgeline, but instead of letting it float freely, the corners need to be fastened to the ridgeline and the tarp pulled tight across the line.

Next, hoist the tarp into the air and tie off the ridgeline tightly. The tarp should be taut across the ridgeline from corner to corner.

Tie off the other two tarp corners to branches or trees, angled down so that water runs off at the corners.

There are other methods of setting up tarps, such as using poles, but the ridgeline method is our favorite. You can use any size tarp and it is fully adjustable to suit your needs.

Using poles is an alternative method if there are not enough or no trees in the immediate area. This setup is not as sturdy as using trees, especially in very windy conditions.

You can use poles cut from the forest, old tent poles, adjustable tarp poles, or anything else you can devise. If you have a truck or roof racks on your car, you can lug a few pieces of lumber along with you for tarp poles. Use small pieces such as 2x3s or 2x2s – drill holes in the ends to attach your ropes.

You need poles long enough to elevate the tarp to an acceptable height so you can walk around underneath. The poles need to be extra-long if you plan to hang the tarp above your fire pit – you don't want the tarp to melt or catch on fire.

You will need sturdy pegs and rope to hold the poles erect, and a ridgeline between the poles to suspend the tarp. Once you have the ridgeline and tarp suspended, you can fasten the remaining corners to ground pegs.

Using a pole to support the centre of the tarp is not a great idea – a ridgeline is best. The pole may puncture a hole in the tarp. If you do have to set your tarp in this manner, use a pole with a flat end and protect the tarp by putting a piece of foam rubber, a towel, etc. on top of the pole.

If you have an extra tarp, you can extend your coverage area by fastening the extra section to your existing tarp setup. This works well in windy conditions to create a lean-to type shelter.

You can tie some of your support lines to your vehicle instead of pegging it down – just don't drive away without untying the lines! Put a note on your steering wheel to remind yourself...

Practice makes perfect. After a few successful tarp setups – and maybe a few failures – you'll be able to do it with relative ease. You'll enjoy staying dry, cooking, and sitting around a warm campfire in the pouring rain, getting the most from your camping experience.

Chapter 4: How to Build A Campfire

"The fire is the main comfort of the camp, whether in summer or winter, and is about as ample at one season as at another. It is as well for cheerfulness as for warmth and dryness." (Henry David Thoreau)

Camping without sitting around a campfire is just not the same. With all the fire bans lately, we try to get in as much camping as possible early in the year before everything dries up and later in the fall when the rains start up again.

There are lots of methods to building and starting a fire, from rubbing two sticks together (never tried that one) to soaking a pile of wood with gasoline or oil (not recommended!), but first of all you need some kind of fire starter.

Fire starters

We prefer to use newspapers and egg cartons, and, for natural starters, birch bark, dried moss, conifer tree resin (kinda sticky), dry pine cones, chunks of resin-rich bark, and "Old Man's Beard" (the green stuff that you find hanging from tree branches). If you use birch bark, or resiny conifer bark, please **don't strip the tree down to the wood** – it can kill the tree – just use the loose bark that is naturally shedding.

It can be difficult to get a fire going after a rain, but you can increase your chances by having some fire starter on hand. You can buy chemical fire starters, or you can make your own ready-to-use starter at home too using these methods:

- Save your clothes dryer lint and spent toilet paper rolls. Stuff the lint inside the rolls. You can wrap them with wax paper to create a wick.

- Place wads of dryer lint, shredded newspaper, sawdust and wood shavings, cotton balls, etc., into the empty cups of an egg carton (or cupcake cases). You can also use a combination of these ingredients. Pour melted paraffin wax over the material, let dry, and cut up into individual sections. You can also melt old, half-burnt candles and crayon pieces.

- You can wrap the above ingredients in sheets of wax paper and twist the ends tight.

*Warning: Use a double boiler method to melt the wax so you don't catch it, and your house, on fire. Place a disposable container, such as an old coffee can, into a pot of water and heat until melted.

- Work petroleum jelly into cotton balls and store them in a tight container.

- Tie pieces of string or yarn to pine cones and dip them into melted wax. Alternately, you can soak the cones in used cooking oil and store in a tight container.

- Save your orange peelings, dry them well, and store up for camping.

If you forgot the fire starter, everything is damp, and you just can't find dry, natural, starter, you could use the following items:

- Lip balm

- Potato chips, Doritos, etc.

- Duct tape

- Hand sanitizer

- Fishing reel oil

- Tea light candles

Building the campfire

If you're camping in a campground, you'll likely have designated fire pits – use them. If you go off wilderness camping, you'll have to make your own. We simply use rocks with raised sections on either side to place our cooking grate.

Think safety first! It's important to find a non-flammable bed for your fire. Fire can spread underground through the roots systems of trees and other plants, igniting a forest fire long after you've made your fire out and left the area.

You need to build your fire pit on bare soil, not dried grass, leaves, or other flammables. If you can't find a fire-proof, sandy or gravely area, dig down to the dirt and clear an area around your fire pit of all flammable materials.

Make a platform using soil, gravel, dirt, and small rocks. Build it up a few inches high and place rocks on top to form your fire pit.

A little extra work on your part could prevent a devastating forest fire. Okay, enough about safety...got it?

You'll need dry firewood. Some people buy bundles, some gather it once they arrive at the campground. If you gather wood, look for downed trees and dead wood – fresh, green trees will not burn well. Also look for dead standing trees – they will be drier than ones lying on damp ground.

*Note: Collecting trees and branches for firewood is prohibited in many government parks.

Buy yourself a good hatchet or small axe for splitting wood into kindling. A good quality saw will enable you to cut down dead trees and saw up pieces of dry wood you find around your campsite. A foldable saw will stow away easily with the sharp blade folded into the handle for safety.

There are several ways to build a campfire. Many people just throw some fire starter in the fire pit on the ground and slowly add tinder, kindling, and firewood. This works well, but there are other methods you may want to try:

The upside-down tier fire

You actually build this fire backwards, or upside-down. We were skeptical about this method the first time we tried it, but it works very well and has become our favourite. Try it!

You build it using tiers, light it up, and it will burn for hours unattended. You won't have to feed the fire – it will burn down and catch the larger pieces on fire all by itself. You can add more wood later for an extended burn.

Start with the biggest pieces of wood you have. Lay two or three pieces on the ground inside your fire pit. Take an additional two or three pieces and cross-pile them on top of the first pieces in the opposite direction.

If you want a bigger, longer-lasting fire, cross-pile more than three pieces per tier and build three or more cross-piled tiers. You can place a frying pan or pot on top of the wood for cooking if you build stable tiers.

Next, take your fire starter and small pieces of tinder (dry leaves, bark, wood shavings, Old Man's Beard, etc.) and place them **on top** of the tiers – you can whittle some shavings with your pocketknife to make tinder. Add some dry, pencil-sized kindling wood (twigs, small branches, larger bark pieces, etc.). Light it up, sit back, and watch the fire spread to the wood below. You don't have to add more wood until your tiers burn down.

The teepee fire

The most common way to light up a campfire is probably the teepee method. It's a good technique for having a small, quick cooking fire, and you are in control of the fire size.

Place your fire starter and tinder on the ground and form a small teepee of kindling all around. Add larger pieces of wood teepee fashion above the small teepee. Light it up, and add more wood as needed.

The lean-to fire

Building a lean-to type structure is another quick and easy way to get your campfire started. It works just as well as the teepee method.

Take a long piece of kindling and stick it securely into the ground at about a 30-degree angle, facing into the wind. You can also lean one end of the kindling on a large piece of wood or against a fire pit rock to create the angle.

Place your starter, tinder, and some small kindling underneath. Lean small pieces of kindling against the support stick on both sides. Lean larger pieces of kindling over the small ones, light it up, and add more wood as necessary.

The Swedish fire-log

Similar to the upside-down fire, and the most interesting campfire method we've seen, it's an excellent way to cook using a cast iron frying pan or Dutch oven. It will also burn for a long time unattended.

Take about five or six split pieces of wood and stand them up on end. Fasten them together with a piece of wire so they will stand freely – you could prop the pieces up using rocks if you don't have wire.

Kindle a fire on top of the pieces and let it burn down into the cracks between the wood. Once the fire is established, place your frying pan on top and cook away.

With any fire, you need to ensure the flames get lots of combustion air. Don't give in to temptation and pile tons of wood onto your little kindling fire. You'll smother it and make it out. Kids are notorious for this...

Leave air gaps in a stone fire pit, with a large opening facing into the prevailing wind.

Fanning the fire will help get it going. We have a fan we bought in Ecuador made from toquilla for fanning a stubborn fire on damp, still days. It works well, but you could use a newspaper, a shingle, or anything else you can find.

Some areas allow gas fireplaces during campfire ban times. We see more of these as fire bans become the norm for summer camping. I suppose a propane fire is better than no fire...

Before you go camping, check for fire bans and, if you're going wilderness camping, check to make sure you can have a fire where you're going and if you need a permit.

Always ensure your campfire is totally, 100% extinguished before leaving your campsite, and always have water available to make it out in case it does catch the woods or grass on fire outside your fire pit.

Keep your fires small, helping to avoid smoldering wood and sparks from drifting into the surrounding woods.

If it's really windy and dry consider not having a fire at all or keep it really small with no sparks.

Chapter 5: Camp Cooking and Favourite Recipes

"Cooking and eating food outdoors makes it taste infinitely better than the same meal prepared and consumed indoors." (Fennel Hudson)

Many people ask what to cook while they are camping. Our answer: "Whatever you want to eat." You can make pizza, cake, pie, casseroles, chili, yummy desserts – almost anything.

You can cook the same things over a campfire or on a propane stove or BBQ as you can at home – you might not bake a lot of bread and pies – but you can. We did make cherry pie once on a tiny charcoal BBQ when we were camped in an orchard picking cherries. It was the best cherry pie we've ever had.

I constructed a makeshift grate out of green tree branches after forgetting our grill. It lasted just long enough to cook our hamburgers before bursting into flames.

Thanksgiving turkey dinner with all the fixin's? You betcha!

Smoked fish is the best over a campfire.

You don't have to eat canned beans, soup, and hotdogs. Use your imagination. Try something different. If your meal is a total failure? Have a good laugh and get out the beans! Make some memories. It doesn't have to be perfect.

This brings to mind the "Flaming Chicken" episode. We were cooking chicken over the fire one afternoon. The whole chicken was in an aluminum tray (one with holes to let the smoke in) and covered with foil wrap. The fat dripping out of the pan caught on fire – so did the chicken. My wife grabbed the oven mitts, picked it up, and started waving it up and down in an effort to extinguish the flames which just it made it burn faster. We still have a good laugh about that one.

You don't need a big propane BBQ or smoker if you don't have the room to pack them. We usually cook over a fire, occasionally use a camp stove, and have a little round charcoal BBQ that we use at times.

Hanging a **Dutch oven** over the campfire or placing it on hot coals is a great way to cook.

A cast iron **pie iron** is an excellent way to make grilled sandwiches, omelets – whatever you can think of for ingredients.

We have cooked **Thanksgiving dinner** several times with our family at the campsite. You need lots of time to keep the fire going at the right temperature, but it's lots of fun – and totally delicious.

To cook a turkey, you'll need a large, aluminum roasting pan. The ones with the holes in the sides will allow smoke to enter, enhancing the flavour. Place the turkey in the pan, season, cover with aluminum foil or another roasting pan, and place it on a sturdy grate over the fire, basting it regularly.

You should use hardwood as it produces long-lasting, hot coals. Get a large, hot fire going and wait until it burns down to a few flames and a big bed of hot coals before you put the turkey on. You'll need to pay attention, adding more small pieces of wood to keep the fire going for a few hours.

You can cook the dressing over the fire if you have a big enough grate, or use a camp stove. After the turkey is partially cooked, add your veggies – potatoes, carrots, parsnips, turnip, onion, etc. Coat the veggies with olive oil using a brush and season with salt, pepper and garlic. Cover and roast with the turkey, turning and basting the veggies occasionally until done.

Smoking fish by the fire is a treat. You'll need at least four or five hours – and maybe a six-pack of beer – for this. Any type of green wood will provide the smoke you need, but apple and alder branches and twigs work very well for smoking fish, giving it a nice flavour. Make sure you have a big pile on hand – you'll need lots.

Start by building a hot fire using dry wood. Have a good bed of hot coals before adding the green wood. To smoke your fish properly, you have to use green, fresh wood – dry wood will produce too much heat and not enough smoke.

You'll need a still day or one with just a slight, steady breeze to ensure the smoke doesn't just blow away in all directions.

Prepare your fish. You can fillet them if you were lucky enough to catch a few big ones, or simply split the small ones so they will lie flat on the grate. Leave the skin attached. If your fillets are thick, score them without cutting the skin so the brine reaches all the meat.

There are lots of recipes for smoking fish. We usually use a very simple **wet brine** with great results:

- Dissolve one cup of salt and one cup of sugar in four cups of water

- You can adjust and personalize the flavour by adding soy sauce, wine, herbs, spices, peppers, and so on – experiment and find your own special recipe.

- Soak the fish in brine for about an hour before you smoke it, preferably in your fridge or cooler

- Take the fish out of the brine and blot it dry with paper towels or newspaper

- Place the fish skin-side down on the grate.

- Pack lots of brown sugar on top of the fish

- Place on your rack and smoke until done – time can vary greatly according to amounts of smoke and heat and the distance of the fish from the fire.

You can use a basting solution instead of packing brown sugar on the fish, spreading the solution on the fish periodically while smoking. We've used a combination of beer, melted butter, salt, and BBQ sauce and it turned out great. Be inventive, experiment – you'll come up with your own favourite recipes.

Another method you can try is **dry brining**:

- Mix one cup of salt and one cup of sugar together with two tablespoons of ground cloves and a few ground bay leaves (or your own favourite herbs and spices)

- Coat the fish thoroughly with this mixture and let sit in a bowl for about an hour or so

- Remove fish from the bowl, rinse with water, and let it dry

- Preferably, let the fish dry overnight in a cool place. If you want to use it right away, blot completely dry before smoking.

- Place skin-side down on the rack and smoke

You need something to hold the fish so that you can stand them up close to the fire. An oven rack works well. Tie the fish to the rack using thin, copper wire to hold it in place. You can also use two racks to sandwich the fish, or any other method you can devise. Long, thin, green twigs woven into the rack will hold the fish in place – or you can make the entire rack out of long twigs. Green wood is supple and won't catch on fire as easily as dry twigs. Use your imagination.

Elevate the fish so that it is in direct contact with the smoke. You want to smoke it slowly, not cook it, so it needs to be away from too much heat. You can use several sticks to fashion a stand. Tie the grate to the sticks on a bit of an angle away from the fire. Sometimes the wind will change direction, so a moveable stand works the best.

Remember – you're not trying to cook the fish, but smoke it slowly over the course of an entire afternoon. Make sure it's not too close to the fire or it will be overcooked and not properly smoked.

How do you tell if it's ready? This is a personal decision. I prefer my fish on the raw side – nice and juicy, but not quite raw. Some people gag at the thought of raw fish, so they want it smoked until firm and cooked. You can take some off the racks when it's still nice and moist and let some smoke until totally firmed up.

Many people smoke fish in small, portable smokers with great results as well. You might want to look into one of these if you plan to smoke fish on a regular basis. You don't need to keep a fire going all afternoon and it is much easier – it's just not as much fun.

We usually cook meats, fish and vegetables over the campfire using a grate. You can use and old BBQ grate, buy a grate, or have one made from stainless steel to suit your needs. You want one that will not rust. Some grates come equipped with legs. Some are adjustable for height. One of our favourites had four thin legs that we adjusted by pushing or pulling in or out of the ground above the fire.

If you BBQ at home, you already know how to cook over a fire – it's just a bit harder to adjust the heat. For best results, you should have hardwood coals, not a roaring blaze. You can add wood as necessary.

Aluminum foil works well for wrapping potatoes and veggies, as does an aluminum pan covered with foil or another pan. We like cooking aluminum-wrapped potatoes and veggies by throwing them directly onto the coals.

Making shish kebabs using green sticks is fun too. We like alternating cubes of tender steak with peppers and onions and cooking it slowly over coals or a low flame.

Breakfast ideas

- Egg muffins. Coat a muffin pan with non-stick oil, add eggs, and cook over a grill on your camp stove or campfire – you can add onions, peppers, etc. for extra flavour. A pie iron works well for this too.

- Potato potpourri. We always make sure to bake extra potatoes so we have some left over for breakfast. Chop them up along with onions, peppers, garlic, tomato, etc., season with salt and pepper, and fry in your cast-iron pan over the fire.

- Pie iron omelets. Mix an egg with a bit of water and empty into your pie iron. Add ingredients (onions, mushrooms, grated cheese, peppers, etc.) to cooker and roast over the fire.

- French toast. Mix up your eggs with milk to make a batter. Dip two pieces of bread into the mixture and place them into your pie iron. Add strawberries or other fruit and cook over your campfire. You can also fry the battered bread and cover with fruit or sauce and whipped cream.

Delicious Desserts

- Orange-peel muffins. Mix up some muffin dough – strawberry, raspberry, lemon, blueberry, etc. Cut a few oranges in half and remove all the rind – you can eat this or strain it for juice. Fill half of the orange halves with muffin dough and cover with the empty halves. Wrap in a couple layers of foil, and place on the grate above the fire or right on top of the hot coals. Turn them often and keep checking until they're cooked.

- Fruit pie. Use any fruit – fresh, canned, or frozen. Place between two slices of buttered bread and cook in your pie iron. You can cover the pie with whipped cream and sprinkle with sugar. You can use piecrust too.

- Stick biscuits. You can make your own dough, or buy some frozen stuff. Spiral-wrap a chunk around a 1-2 inch diameter stick that has been whittled clean at the end, and roast over the campfire until thoroughly baked. Fill with whatever you have on hand – chocolate, jam or jelly, peanut butter, syrup – or just eat as is. Make them for breakfast using cheese, ham and eggs, syrup, or bacon.

- Roasted apples. Core a few apples and fill with basically anything sweet. A mixture of brown sugar and cinnamon, Nutella, fruit jam or jelly – use your imagination. Wrap in foil and throw onto hot coals or cook on your grate until soft – check with a fork or toothpick.

Bread and cakes

- Mix up your favourite cake recipe at home and put in a container – or just do it at the campsite. You could try a fruity upside down cake too. Ready your fire so you have lots of hot coals. Put your cake mix in a Dutch oven and cover. Place on top of the hot coals and put lots of coals on top of the lid. Move some coals to surround the pot. Bake until ready. You can make pies using this method too.

- You can bake a loaf of bread on a campfire too. Cover the bottom of your Dutch oven with small stones to make a level platform. Place foil on top of the stones, add your favourite dough mixture, and cover. Place oven on top of a few hot coals, and add coals on top of the lid. Tongs come in handy here. Be sure to put more coals on top of the lid than at the bottom of the pot. Bake until done. Enjoy warm with butter and jam. Yum! Pizza is great cooked this way too.

Main meals

- Campfire quesadillas. Cook your veggie ingredients, such as onions, corn, and mushrooms, wrapped in foil over the campfire – or sauté using a frying pan and camp stove. Place tortillas on large pieces of foil. Sprinkle grated cheese on tortillas, add veggie mix, add more cheese. Fold the tortillas together and wrap totally in foil. Cook over the campfire on a grate until the cheese is melted. Mmmmm.

- Sloppy Joes. Precook the hamburger and drain any fat. Mix it with diced onions, garlic, BBQ sauce, and season to taste. Place between buttered bread in a pie iron and cook until toasted.

- Dutch oven goodies. Use your favourite chili recipe and cook it slowly over the campfire. Make macaroni and cheese, nachos, your favourite stew, soups and chowders – whatever you make at home. You can place the Dutch oven on the grate or hang it over the fire.

- Pizza. Yes, you can make pizza on your campfire. You'll need a good, hot bed of coals first, adding a few small pieces of firewood as needed. Place a clean grate over the fire and test it for heat – if you can hold your hand over the grate for about 10 seconds, you're ready to cook your pizza. Adjust the grate height accordingly. Place the pizza dough on the grate and cook until browned. Flip it over and add your favourite ingredients. Cover the pizza with a pan or foil and cook until ready. A little experimentation and experience and you'll be cooking excellent pizza pies!

- Pie iron pizza. Place a piece of dough in the iron. Add sauce and your favourite toppings. Cover with another piece of dough. Roast over the fire for about five minutes per side until cooked.

- Corn-on-the-cob is delicious cooked on the campfire too. Soak the corn with husks in water for an hour or so. Place directly on hot coals until cooked. Alternately, cook on the grate above the fire wrapped in foil.

- Steamed mussels and clams are a super appetizer. Just put the shellfish in a pot and cook over the fire until they start steaming. Wait until the shells open and enjoy.

- Lobsters, shrimp, crabs, and prawns can be cooked over hot coals too. Get a really hot fire going and burn down until you have a big bed of coals. Gather some rockweed (the stuff with the little pockets of water on it) from the shore and throw on the coals. Place the lobsters on top and steam until cooked. If you don't have access to rockweed, cook them in a pot of salt water.

Snacks

- S'mores. Number one on the snack list, of course. Roast a marshmallow over the fire until browned all around. Sandwich the hot marshmallow between two graham crackers along with a piece of chocolate. You can use a biscuit instead of crackers and add strawberries. Try adding peanut butter. Chocolate chip and peanut butter cookies work well too. Be creative.

- You can make a wide variety of snacks with your pie iron. Cover two slices of bread with lots of peanut butter. Place marshmallows and a piece of chocolate bar on the bread. Toast in the pie iron until the chocolate has melted and the bread is toasted.

Pie iron notes: When making sandwiches in your cooker, butter the bread slices and place the buttered sides against the cast iron so it doesn't stick. When adding ingredients such as eggs, dough, etc. directly to the pie iron, grease the sides well to prevent sticking. You can get pretty creative using a pie iron – experiment with something different on each camping trip.

You can use charcoal briquettes or a gas BBQ instead of lighting a wood fire to cook some of these recipe ideas if you prefer.

So now you have an idea of what you can eat while camping – basically anything you put your mind to making. Experiment and have fun!

Chapter 6: Fun Family Camping

"We didn't realize we were making memories, we just knew we were having fun." (Winnie the Pooh)

Surprisingly, many people have expressed concerns about camping with their children. Will they be bored? What will they do without an internet connection? What will we do to keep them occupied? Can we take our baby camping? Many questions and concerns that just never crossed our minds – we just packed up, went to a campsite, and had fun.

Camping has resulted in some of our best family memories, so a chapter dedicated to family camping seems appropriate. I've put together some of the things we did with our children to help you out and maybe put your mind at ease.

Driving to your campsite can be the worst part of the trip. Kids get bored quickly and a long drive can become an ordeal. We played games on longer drives, such as counting red cars, counting cows, counting anything.

Play an alphabet game – start with "A" and get your kids to try to spot something beginning with each letter. You probably won't get through the entire alphabet before they tire of it, but we found it a fun way to occupy an hour or so of driving time.

Our kids used to put things on my head as I was driving – napkins, chips, French fries, stuffed animals – I pretended not to notice. Things would fall off my head and I'd ask them what they were laughing about. This kept them – and us – occupied for long stretches – it doesn't take much to entertain children.

Company for your child is important, especially if they are an only child. They love to play with friends –

consider inviting one or two of their best buds along for the trip or, even better, invite the whole family to camp in the site next door. You'll also have someone to compare notes with…

Kids like having their own **separate and private space**. You can help them build a "fort" in the woods with downed trees and branches. Bring an extra small tent along for them to play in and maybe sleep in too. A simple tent made from blankets or sleeping bags hung over a rope is fascinating for kids – they can make a little house and play inside for hours.

You can take your baby with you! Yes, you can. We did and it was great. Our son was born in January and was only four months old when he experienced his first May long weekend camping trip – and he still loves camping.

We bought a small, inflatable swimming pool and used it for a crib - no worries about him rolling out. A yard sale yielded a small hammock. We hung it between two trees, tied a long rope to it, and gave the rope a pull once in a while to keep it swinging. He slept like a baby. Well, I guess he was a baby…

Children need entertainment while camping – outdoor entertainment. Here are a few things we found entertaining for both the kids and us:

- Water is a child magnet. Show them water and they will play for hours. We usually camped by the ocean or a lake with our kids. They would swim and play for hours on the beach or lakeshore.

- Some campgrounds have swimming pools for family enjoyment.

- If you have an air mattress, your children can use it for a boat. **Wind will blow an air mattress**

out into the water quickly so you have to be vigilant or tie it to the shore.

- Hiking along the lake or sea shore, through the forest, anywhere... Seashell and rock collections were common on our picnic table and inside our tent.

- Make sure to pack plenty of snacks – all their faves.

- Roasting marshmallows and hot dogs is sure to keep them occupied for an hour or so each day.

- Playgrounds are found in most campgrounds and can keep your kids entertained for at least a short time.

- Books – bring lots of books for reading and colouring.

- Set up a live squirrel trap. Use a cardboard box, a plastic container, whatever you have on hand. Prop one end up with a stick, tie a long string to the stick, and put some bait, such as peanuts or peanut butter, under the trap. Wait patiently for a squirrel to take the bait – pull the string and catch the squirrel! I don't think they ever actually caught one, but the kids spent hours having a great time trying.

- Fishing is another activity that kids love – they don't have much patience and continuously get the line snarled and cast their hooks in trees, but it's great when they catch a fish.

- Any outdoor game will work – croquet, washer-toss, horseshoes, lawn darts, a bubble maker, glow sticks for nighttime fun, or just throwing a baseball or Frisbee.

- Make a game out of gathering firewood, play hide-and-seek, organize a scavenger hunt – or just make something up and add rules as you go.

- If you're in a wooded area, stash candies or prizes in various locations around the campsite. Draw a "treasure map" giving clues as to where the booty is hidden. Your kids will have a great time finding their treats. Make it really difficult if you want a longer break…

- We always took our bicycles. Most campground roads are safe for biking and many have biking trails.

- Pack rain gear, umbrellas, and lots of extra clothing. Don't let a little rain ruin the fun. Kids love water and they enjoy playing in the rain and the puddles. Let them enjoy it and get wet and dirty.

Teach your children to value and respect nature and the Great Outdoors. Show them – set an example – that there is more to life than the world of electronics.

They love to explore. They need to learn to enjoy the pleasures that abound in nature. If you teach them, they'll love it for the rest of their lives.

Chapter 7: Camping With Pets

"Our perfect companions never have fewer than four feet." (Colette)

We've taken several cats camping. They all seemed to hate camping, and we've had bad luck with our cats. We may never go cat-camping again...

Our first cat-camping trip resulted in a dead cat. He decided to curl up in the radiator shroud of a friend's car – he started his car...

Our second trip with a cat resulted in a runaway. We were driving back to Nova Scotia from Prince Rupert, BC via the North American coastline. We camped on a beach in Oregon and woke up in the morning discovering our beloved cat was missing. I followed his tracks down the beach for miles but never caught up with him. We figured he had enough of being trapped in the car – hope he made it to California!

We bought a harness for our third cat-camping episode. She hated it! She spent most of her time slinking around on her belly – she was not used to being tied.

Deciding that it would be better for our cats, we left them at home. We made sure they had lots of water and food to last until we got home – and two clean litter boxes. If we were gone for more than a few nights, we had someone come in to take care of them.

If you're a cat owner, you know how finicky they can be. Every cat is different – some are scared to death of everything, others just don't care.

If you do decide to take your cats on a camping trip, consider the following advice:

- Use a soft-sided, collapsible carrier for the car trip – you don't want an escapee when you stop for a break. The carrier can double for a bed and a safe retreat too.

- Buy a proper harness – one that they cannot escape from – and a retractable leash

- Accustom your cat to the harness and leash long before you get to the campsite

- Bring along your cat's bed and favourite toys

- If your cat is strictly an indoor kitty bring along his familiar litter box

- Do a trial run. Set the tent up in the back yard or in your house and get your cat accustomed to it before the first camping trip.

- Buy a collar with LED lights to make finding your cat easier in the dark in case she does escape.

- Attach an ID tag with your address and phone number, and consider microchipping.

- If you plan to go on long hikes, you'll need to carry your cat – unless he happens to be a rare cat that loves to walk for miles on a leash. Don't leave him alone at the campsite – he may panic, try everything to escape, and have a totally traumatic camping experience. Buy a backpacking kitty carrier and take him with you.

If you're lucky, your cat will love camping and you'll take her with you wherever you go. She may be OK after several trips and decide that camping is not that bad. On the other hand, she may simply hate it, making your cat-camping experience less than enjoyable. You may decide to leave her at home where she feels safe and comfortable.

Dogs, on the other hand, totally enjoy a camping trip. It's dog heaven – hiking, swimming, all the scents – squirrels! Our dogs just loved camping. As soon as we started packing up the truck they were inside waiting – and in the way of our packing.

We've always taken our dogs camping and have had nothing but good experiences – well, except once. I hope you see the humour in this story as we do.

Both of our dogs ate something that gave them a severe case of diarrhea – and I mean brutal. I took the youngest for a walk just after sunrise the next morning.

Several hammock-campers were hanging in the trees, close to the roadway in a campsite near ours. The diarrhea-storm struck just feet away from the nearest hammock – a liquid, steaming stream shooting straight out for several feet.

The smell was horrendous! How do you clean it up? Well, you just can't. We got out of there as quickly as possible as the hammock started moving…maybe they thought it was a bear?

Anyhow…hopefully this never happens to your dogs. Keep a close eye on them on your walks and don't let them eat anything.

Following are some general tips and advice to consider before you pack up for your camping trip:

- Make sure the campground you are going to is dog friendly – most are, but there are a few that don't allow pets or have size and breed limits.

- On the drive to the campsite, stop regularly for a short bathroom/exercise breaks and give them lots of water to drink.

- Treat your dog with a tick and flea medication and check often for ticks during your trip. A tick remover tool will come in handy if you do run into a tick-infested area.

- Ensure Lyme disease, rabies, and other vaccinations are up-to-date.

- Make sure there is some type of identification tag with your address and phone number fastened to your dog's collar in case he decides to run off. Microchipping is also an option.

- Pack things your dogs are familiar with so they feel at home – toys, favourite blanket, whatever they love the most. Dogs get bored too. A good dog bone can keep them occupied for hours and playing with a ball, stick, or Frisbee makes them happy.

- If you are crossing international borders be sure to check regulations and have the necessary paperwork with you.

- Pack an extra collar, an extendable leash, and a piece of rope to make a run (details on how to make a run below).

- Pack water bottles and a treat container for hiking.

Keep your dog on a leash. We've walked hundreds of kilometres with our dogs, always keeping them leashed.

Some people are positive their dogs are perfect and wouldn't harm a flea. Even the friendliest dogs in the world can bite if they feel threatened by kids or other dogs. It's pretty scary to have an unleashed, large-breed dog run up to you or your children while hiking or into your campsite.

Be considerate and leash your pet around other dogs and people, and remember that some people simply don't like animals and are terrified of dogs.

Leashing your dog could also help avoid encounters with wildlife, such as bears, wolves, skunks, porcupines, coyotes, or cougars (cougars will eat a small dog for a snack). A skunk encounter will make for very unpleasant sleeping arrangements.

Always carry doggy bags with you so nobody has the misfortune of stepping in your dog's poo. If you forget bags, make sure to remove the poop from any beaches and trails and bury it in nearby woods or bushes, covering it thoroughly with branches, leaves, or rocks.

Dogs enjoy guarding the campsite. We've always kept our dogs tied, and tried to keep them in back so they don't scare other people when they walk by our campsite. One of our dogs loved to lie in wait and ambush people when they walked by...

A method we found that works great and gives the dogs running space is to stretch a rope between two trees. Make sure there is a shady spot if it's hot.

Elevate it to a height so you won't strangle yourself or your kids when they walk up to it, or leave it lying on the ground. Elevated is best so you don't trip on the line.

Tie it tightly using knots that are easily adjusted and untied – refer to the chapter on knots and learn how to tie a few.

Tie a clip to another piece of rope so that you can easily clip and unclip the line to the dog's collar. Make the rope long enough so that your dog can lie down with a bit of slack in the line.

Tie a bowline around the main run line to form a loop that will slide along the rope. You can also tie stops in the main line so that they can't get wrapped around the tree trunks.

Note: Make sure there is enough slack in the line so that your dog isn't hung by jumping off an embankment or a hollow in the ground. In addition, keep a constant watch to make sure they aren't tangled and choking and never leave them alone while tied.

If you happen to have a large area, you can use a rope tied to a stake in the middle of the open area – you won't have to worry about your dog getting wrapped around trees and bushes.

Some people prefer to bring portable, folding fencing units with them.

Please don't let your dog bark every time someone walks by your campsite and repeat yourself telling him to be quiet. We've heard neighbours continuously tell their dogs to be quiet – all day and night. It's annoying – be considerate – remember that everyone doesn't love your dog as much as you do, no matter how cute she is. A constantly barking dog is about as annoying as a perpetually running generator.

We actually had neighbours leave their dog locked up in their camper while they spent a few hours on the beach. The poor dog barked the entire time they were gone!

Our dogs always sleep in the tent with us. We make up a comfy bed on the floor using familiar bedding they sleep on at home. Somehow they always end up on the bed with us or our children anyway and take up the whole bed…

Take precautions so that your pets can't escape the tent in the middle of the night. We've awoken in the morning to find our dogs gone. They found their way out through the zippered door in our tent. We found them roaming through the campground, looking for snacks no doubt. We had to block off the zippered sections with storage boxes after that…

We hope you and your dog enjoy camping as much as we have. Our dogs are no longer with us physically, but

their memories live on during all our camping trips –
and every time we see a hammock camper, we just
have to chuckle…

Chapter 8: Roughing It (Primitive Toilets and Showers)

"I've learned that life is like a roll of toilet paper. The closer it gets to the end, the faster it goes." (Andy Rooney)

We all need to relieve ourselves and stay clean – well, relatively clean – when camping. If you like all the bathroom comforts-of-home, such as flush toilets and hot showers, check to be sure that the campground you choose has these facilities. Some do not.

Many campgrounds have pit or vault toilets only and no shower facilities. We usually don't mind vault toilets, but a few have been smelly and dirty.

Wilderness campsites often have no toilet facilities whatsoever. You'll need to be prepared.

Toilets are important – simple as that. For primitive pooping, a small shovel will come in handy for digging holes and covering up. If you don't have a shovel, you can make a small depression by moving vegetation, squat over your spot, and cover up after you've finished.

For a bit more comfort, find a downed tree about the right height for a seat, dig a hole, sit on the log, and cover up thoroughly. Not a problem.

For a bit more luxury, a 5-gallon bucket will work. You can make your own comfy toilet by adding a seat and lid to a bucket or buy a ready-made bucket toilet kit.

To make your own, you'll need a 5-gallon bucket with a tight-fitting lid, a toilet seat with a cover, a piece of exterior-grade ¾-inch plywood, exterior-grade adhesive caulking, a few short screws, and maybe a bit of paint.

Note: You need to find a toilet seat and cover assembly that will fit flat onto a piece of plywood. You need one that you can remove the bumper/cushion pads from the seat, and one that does not have the cover hinges screwed to the bottom of the seat.

Here's how to make your own porta-bucket toilet:

- First of all, you need a hole in the plywood. Start by tracing the top of the bucket (with the lid off) on your piece of plywood – place the bucket upside-down on the plywood.

- Cut out the hole in the plywood – make sure the hole is big enough so that the plywood slides onto the top of the bucket.

- Remove the cushion/bumper pads from the bottom of the toilet seat – you want a flat surface with no protuberances. This is why you need a cover that is not fastened to the underside of the seat.

- Place the seat onto the plywood, centering it over the hole in the plywood. Trace the seat outline onto the plywood.

- Cut the shape of the seat from the plywood. You'll end up with a piece of plywood the same size as the toilet seat with a hole in middle.

- Sand the cut edges of the plywood smooth and apply a couple coats of exterior, gloss paint – you want to make cleaning as easy as possible.

- Fasten the plywood to the seat with an exterior grade adhesive and a few screws (make sure the screws are the right length so they don't penetrate all the way through the seat). Lay the seat upside down on a stable work surface. Drill pilot holes for the screws. Put a coat of adhesive on the seat and screw the seat to the plywood.

- You can now place this assembly on the bucket, with the hole in the plywood sliding down over the bucket top so it doesn't slide off.

- When you finish using the bucket, install the tight-fitting lid to transport your bucket for emptying.

Add kitty litter or wood shavings and sawdust (cedar works well) before and after usage. You can dig deep disposal holes nearby, covering up as your camping trip goes by.

Eventually, you'll need to clean your bucket toilet. Keep this in mind when making your own or buying a portable model. Lining the bucket with a biodegradable liner bag will make cleanup much easier.

Cutting the bottom out of the bucket is an option. You can dig holes each time you use it, covering up each time. This negates the problem of what to do when the bucket fills up and lessens the odour factor.

People are very creative with outdoor toilets. They've been made with milk crates, plastic lawn chairs, pool noodles fastened to a bucket – lots of ideas to make pooping in the woods a bit more enjoyable.

For total luxury – and especially in the pouring rain – you could buy a small outhouse tent for privacy to house your bucket toilet or portable toilet if you have extra room in your vehicle and can pack everything in to the campsite.

There are many tent and toilet options available. Small privacy tents are readily available, and many options exist for portable toilets, including composting models.

Campground showers can be pretty sketchy at times. We've come across some pretty gross shower stalls. Wearing flip-flops or sandals while taking a shower in less than clean showers makes us feel a little better.

Some places are free; some require coins and can be expensive – and you could run out of coins in the middle of your shower – a real pain. Check out the facility details before you decide on a campground.

If you are in the wilderness, you can fashion your own shower, buy a solar-heated shower bag or other portable unit, or just bathe in a creek or lake.

Heating up some water and taking a sponge bath is a possibility as well.

You can make your own shower and toilet privacy enclosure using a tarp tied to a few trees. If you already have a toilet privacy tent, you can take your portable toilet out while you use it as a shower.

Most people want warm water for their shower. You can heat water by filling a black container and placing it the sun; you can circulate water through your campfire using copper tubing; you can heat it up in a pot and pour it into your improvised shower water container, such as a bucket with holes drilled in the bottom – or whatever other method you can devise.

Getting the water up to the overhead shower outlet can be achieved using a 12-volt pump connected to a power outlet in your vehicle.

I like the DIY garden sprayer shower. It's simple to make, lightweight and portable, and its pressurized so you don't need to hang it above your shower enclosure to use it.

Here's how to make your porta-shower:

- Buy a new garden sprayer – you don't want to reuse one that has had chemicals run through it. Buy the largest one you can find. You can paint it black to heat the water using the sun.

- Remove the existing wand from the sprayer and replace it with a garden hose nozzle.

- If the existing garden sprayer hose is too short, replace it with a longer section of tubing or garden hose.

- Fill the tank with a mixture of two parts cold water and one part boiling-hot water – or adjust to the temperature you prefer.

- Pump up the garden sprayer to pressurize and you're ready to shower.

- Note: You could improvise further by using a showerhead with a built-in shutoff valve and fasten it overhead – to a tree, for example – for hands-free showers.

You can improvise on your toiletry equipment over the years until you have the perfect setup. Be creative and have fun!

Chapter 9: Learn How to Tie a Few Basic Knots

"When you reach the end of your rope, tie a knot in it and hang on." (Franklin D. Roosevelt)

Before you head out on your camping trip, learn how to tie a few knots. You'll be able to secure your tarp lines, fasten your tent stays, put up a clothesline, make a running line for your pets – and impress your friends.

You'll be able to untie these lines without cutting them off and leaving ropes and strings hanging in the tree branches. Practice until you can tie them handily.

It's difficult to explain a knot rather than showing someone in person. Videos showing how to tie knots are readily available online for visual instruction. We've included a few with diagrams to get you started.

These basic, easy-to-tie knots should get you by on a camping trip. There are so many more, and lots of instructional books and online videos are available to help you tie the more difficult knots.

You can download these **two free knot books** available through "Project Gutenberg":

"Knots, Splices and Rope Work", by A. Hyatt Verrill

http://www.gutenberg.org/ebooks/13510

"Knots, Bends, Splices", by Captain Jutsum

http://www.gutenberg.org/ebooks/30983

Following, you'll find a few basic knots that will come in handy. The diagrams (taken from the above free knot books) will help you figure out how to tie them. Have fun and practice until you can easily tie them all.

- **Bowline:** You can use this handy knot in many situations. You can put as much tension on this knot as you want and it will still untie easily. Start by making a small loop. Pass the free end of the rope under and up through the loop. Continue the end around the back of the line and down through the loop. Tighten. **Uses:** Make a sliding loop to use as a dog lead; tie lines to your tarp.

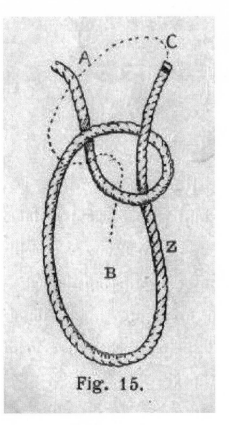

Fig. 15.

Fig. 16.

- **Double half hitch:** A very simple knot to learn – not much instruction needed beyond the diagram below. **Uses:** Tie a rope to a tree; fasten a line to a loop in another line.

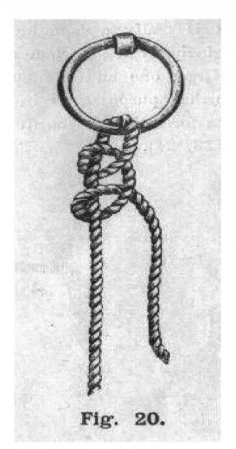

Fig. 20.

- **Clove hitch:** To make this knot, pass the end of rope around the tree, then over itself; over and around the tree, and pass the end under itself and between the rope and tree, as shown in the illustration. To make the clove hitch more secure, add a half hitch with the free end of the rope. **Use:** Fasten a line to a tree trunk or branch.

FIG. 36 *A.*—Clove hitch or builder's hitch (tying).

FIG. 36 *B.*—Clove hitch (complete).

- **Square knot:** Eventually, you will need to join two pieces of rope to make a longer piece. The square knot is strong, never slips or becomes jammed, and is easily untied. Take the ends of the rope and pass the left end over and under the right end. Next, pass the right end over and under the left. Remember: "Left over," "Right over," and you'll never make a mistake and form the useless Granny knot which is not easily untied. Refer to the diagram below, and be sure end "a" is kept in front of part "b", and the other end follows the direction of the dotted line. When the knot is finished correctly, it should look like Fig. 49 in the diagram. **Use:** Tie two pieces of line together for extra length.

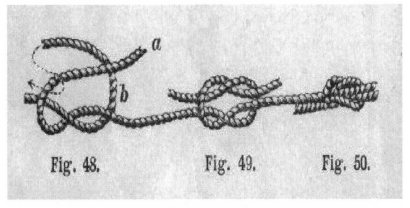

Fig. 48.   Fig. 49.   Fig. 50.

- **Sheet bend:** Another easily untied knot for joining two pieces of rope. Refer to the following diagram and make a small loop with one rope. Pass the second rope's end underneath the eye and bring up through the loop. Next, pass the end around the back of the first rope and back under itself. It will hold better and is less likely to jamb if it passed around again as in Fig. 53. **Use:** Join two pieces of line.

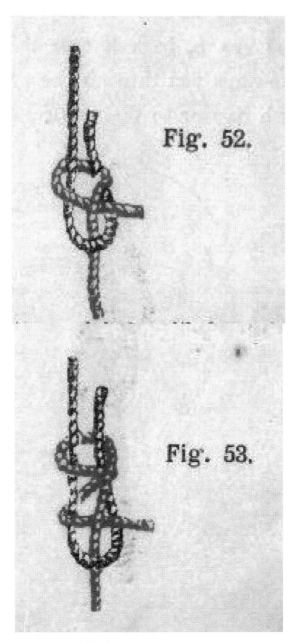

Fig. 52.

Fig. 53.

- **Slippery hitch:** This is simple to tie and very easy to untie. To make this knot, pass the end of the rope through the ring or eye to which it is being fastened. Bring it back over the standing part, making a loop. To untie, simply pull on the free end. **Use:** Fasten a line to any loop or ring.

FIG. 32.—Slippery hitch
(complete).

FIG. 33 —Slippery hitch
(tying).

Practice these knots until you can tie them with your eyes closed – you'll be glad you did. You will never struggle to untie a knot again, and won't have to cut all your lines when you leave the campsite. Once you master these, learn a few more super-complicated, fancy knots to impress your friends.

Chapter 10: Bears, Cougars, and Other Dangerous Stuff

"What on earth would I do if four bears came into my camp? Why, I would die of course. Literally shit myself lifeless." (Bill Bryson, A Walk in the Woods)

While seldom seen, wild animals do exist in almost all regions. They are unpredictable and can be dangerous. You need to take this seriously, especially if you plan to camp and hike in wilderness areas.

Bears!

What would you do if you encountered a bear? Would you be prepared?

Bears can appear in an instant and will usually run away from people. But what if they don't run away – what would you do if one charged you?

They can be dangerous if surprised, especially if you happen to end up between momma-bear and her cubs. We've had the good fortune to see several bears on our hiking and camping trips, but have never been attacked or threatened.

We watched a bear walk along a beach with her two cubs on a popular seaside trail in Thomas Raddall Park, Nova Scotia. We saw a bear run up a set of stairs on a popular trail – just behind a group of hikers – in Forillon National Park in Quebec. While leaving a campground early one morning in Ontario, we watched a bear run through a group of tents. A bear splashed its way along a brook – right next to us – while walking a trail in Powell River, British Columbia. Yup, they are out there, and the more time you spend in the woods, the more likely you are to have a close encounter.

Before you go on your next camping trip, pack bear spray, and learn how to use it. Check park web pages for information about bears in the area. Look for bear notices when you arrive at your campground.

Don't attract animals to your campsite with human and pet food, garbage, dirty camp stoves, toilet areas, or other smelly items. Ensure things are locked away in a metal bear-proof container, in your car, or hung from a tree away from your campsite – not in your tent.

Use designated campground areas to dispose of dishwater or choose a place far away from your campsite.

While out hiking, make lots of noise so you don't surprise a bear, especially in areas of limited visibility, on windy days, or close to babbling brooks and streams. You could sing, clap your hands once in a while, talk loudly, blow a whistle, wear noisy bear bells – anything to let the bears know you're coming their way.

Be on the lookout for bear tracks and scat. Note any strange smells, disturbed vegetation, and overturned rocks and logs.

If you're walking into the wind, your scent will be blown behind you so make extra noise.

Hike in groups when possible and don't let your children wander off the trail.

Dogs can provoke a bear into attacking – keep your dog leashed.

If you do encounter a bear, remain calm – at least try not to panic and do not run. (If you do run, first make sure you're not the slowest person in the group...)

All joking aside, don't provoke an attack. If the bear has not seen you, sneak away quietly – move while its head is down if it's feeding. If it does see you, talk in a low, calm voice – don't yell and try to scare it away. Don't stare into its eyes – this could be interpreted as a challenge.

Back up slowly and don't turn your back on the bear. If it follows you, try to distract it by dropping something on the ground – a backpack or some other item. Make sure you're not blocking the bear's path or standing between it and any cubs.

Standing up on its hind legs does not mean the bear is attacking – it's just getting a better look at you and trying to smell you. If the bear looks directly at you with its head lowered and ears laid back on its head, it could be ready to attack.

Remember this – bears can run faster than you, they can swim, and they can climb trees – and they can run fast downhill too.

If the bear approaches or charges – do not run! Use your bear spray when it's close enough. If the bear does make contact with you, try to roll onto your stomach. If you are being stalked by a bear, which is a rare occurrence, it probably sees you as prey and may attack. If it does, use your spray.

If you are attacked, the strategies for black and grizzly bears differ. Is it a black bear or a grizzly? Learn to tell the difference and know what type of bears live in the area. Someone mentioned this to me while we were talking about bear safety: "If it's black, fight back. If it's brown, lie down."

Note: Playing dead is a controversial topic. Some seasoned experts tell you to never play dead in any situation, others say it's the only thing you should do. Playing dead is a personal choice that you will hopefully never have to make.

Black bears: Stand your ground, stand tall, make lots of noise, and wave your arms in the air. Fight back! Use any object you have – sticks, rocks, camera, fists, whatever. If you're absolutely positive the attacking bear is a mother protecting her cubs, play dead.

Grizzly bears: Play dead. Lie face down on the ground and cover the back of your neck with your hands. Try not to move. Spread your legs apart for stability to remain on your stomach. Stay quiet and still until the bear leaves – they will sometimes watch you and come back if they see movement. If it decides to start eating you, you must fight back – concentrate on the face, nose, and eyes.

The best strategy is avoiding an encounter – let the bears know you're in the area so they can move away.

Cougars!

These large, powerful cats are stealthy and seldom seen by hikers. They hunt at all times, but are mostly active between dusk and dawn. They pose the biggest danger to small children and pets.

Take the same precautions as with bears – let them know you're in the area. If you do see a cougar, don't make any sudden movements or run away! Face it and stand tall.

If a cougar does advance on you, pick up small pets and children, maintain eye contact with the cougar, make yourself look big, yell loudly – try to scare it away. If it does attack, throw rocks and sticks and fight back.

Wolves and coyotes!

Take the same precautions as with bears – avoid confrontation. If you do have a close encounter with a wolf or coyote, act the same as you would a cougar. Don't run or turn your back, if they advance try to scare them away, and in case of attack fight back.

Ticks and Lyme disease!

So – you've found a place where there are no bears, cougars, wolves, coyotes – nothing that's going to eat you. You're totally safe, right? Not quite!

Even tiny creatures like ticks can be harmful. Some species of ticks carry Lyme disease that can become a very serious health problem.

Lyme disease is caused by bacteria and is spread through the bites of infected ticks. Ticks that carry Lyme disease are the blacklegged or deer tick. These ticks are much smaller than the typical dog tick – about the size of a sesame seed or smaller.

Try to find out if the area you are visiting is a high-risk tick and Lyme disease zone before you go.

Prevent ticks from getting on your clothing and skin. Use the following precautionary methods:

- When you go on a hike, try to stay on wide paths and avoid bushes and tall grass. *Note: We have noticed that if we walk through ferns, we get no ticks on us at all. Ferns also seem to repel horseflies – stick a piece in your hair or hat.

- Wear light-coloured pants and long-sleeved shirts so that any ticks will show up more easily and you can pick them off as you go.

- Keep your shirt tucked into your pants, and your pants tucked into your socks to make it harder for the little beasts to reach your skin.

- Apply an insect repellent containing DEET or Icaridin to your clothing and exposed skin.

- After hiking, do a tick check – check everything including pets and hiking gear. The sooner you remove a tick from your skin, the better –

removal within 24-36 hours usually prevents infection.

- Check your clothes and hair. Strip down and check all areas of your skin. You can do this with your partner to make it more interesting...

If you find a tick and it has fastened itself to your skin, don't panic and yank it off – you don't want to leave its mouth parts under your skin.

You can buy a tick removal tool or just use fine-tipped tweezers. Grip the tick by the head or as close to the skin as possible and ease it out with steady and even pressure. Don't use a jerking or twisting motion.

Clean the area and your hands with rubbing alcohol.

Follow up. If you develop a rash or fever within a few weeks, contact your doctor immediately. Lyme disease can be treated with antibiotics.

Poison Ivy, Poison Oak, and Poison Sumac!

Yes, even a few plants can be harmful. Poison Ivy, Oak, and Sumac won't attack and eat you, but you can develop a very uncomfortable, itchy rash, hives, or blisters to totally ruin your camping trip.

Learn to recognize these plants and stay away. Look for signs in campgrounds and along hiking trails indicating their presence.

If you are exposed to any of these plants, wash your skin with cool, soapy water or rubbing alcohol. If a rash does develop, several treatments can be used to alleviate the symptoms:

- Include calamine lotion in your first aid kit and apply to relieve itching
- Apply cold water and cold cloth compresses

- If you experience an anaphylactic reaction, go to the nearest emergency department ASAP. Some people experience trouble breathing, eyelids swelling shut, or swelling of the genitals (yikes!).

Please don't be discouraged after reading this chapter! It sounds worse than it really is, for sure. Take the proper precautions and you'll do just fine. We've been camping and hiking since the '70s and haven't had a serious problem yet.

We've never seen a cougar – but I do hope to see one in the wild during my lifetime.

The only grizzly bear we've ever seen was in Waterton National Park, Alberta on a bear-watching/camping trip in September – and it was a safe distance away and not the least bit interested in us.

We have spotted quite a few black bears, but they've always decided to run away. Some were very close but caused us no problems.

The only wolf I've ever seen was a friend's pet wolf – we used to play Frisbee in the park with him.

We've seen a few coyotes but have never had a problem with them either.

Sightings of dangerous, wild animals are rare – consider yourself lucky if you do see them. **Attacks are very rare!** Don't be afraid to enjoy the Great Outdoors.

Be prepared. Make sure to reduce the possibility of encounters. Know what to do if a close encounter happens. If you are nervous, camp in places with other people and hike in groups.

Just be sure to get outside and enjoy yourselves!

Chapter 11: How to Choose a Flashlight or Headlamp

"Flashlight: A mechanical device used by people to carry around dead batteries." (Anonymous)

We don't know who came up with this definition, but we can relate to it. A dependable flashlight is a camping necessity. This chapter will help you choose a flashlight that's right for you – and more than just a dead battery holder.

With thousands of flashlights on the market, deciding on the right one can be overwhelming. Do you need a super-bright light? Do you want long-lasting performance for multi-day hikes? You may need a tactical model with a blinding strobe setting for protection from an attacker while out walking at night. Do you want a flashlight with built-in rechargeable batteries and variable power settings?

Performance ratings

Look for a flashlight indicating ANSI FL1 ratings. These standards ensure models are tested and rated in the same way. The following list describes some of the qualities you should check out before deciding on a new flashlight.

Output

The intensity of the light produced by a flashlight measured in **lumens**. This rating is sometimes shown for multiple light settings available on models with variable outputs.

Beam distance

Measured in metres, this rating determines the distance of illumination before the brightness diminishes to the equivalent of the light from a full moon.

Impact resistance

Measured in metres, this test ensures the flashlight will still work after being repeatedly dropped onto a concrete floor.

Water resistance

Waterproof flashlights are a must, especially if you're a hiker, camper, or fisherman. Three ratings are used to demonstrate waterproof rankings, with testing performed after impact testing. An IPX4 rated flashlight is simply splash-resistant; IPX7 lights are good for temporary water immersion for up to 30 minutes at a depth of 1m; an IPX8 rated flashlight can withstand submersion for up to 4 hours at the specified depth.

Run-time

The measurement in hours of how long it takes the amount of light produced by the flashlight to drop to 10% of the rated output (using new batteries). Sometimes represented by a graph, this measure is commonly given for each light setting available with the tested unit. Smaller, single-battery flashlights generally have shorter run times. Larger lights with specialized rechargeable batteries last longer – some up to several days on low power settings.

Brightness

Don't be fooled by false advertising. A $10 flashlight advertised as having an output of 10,000 lumens? I don't think so. A more expensive, top-quality flashlight with an output of 1000 lumens is a realistic figure.

Remember – when comparing flashlights, it's important to check that the lumen rating follows the ANSI FL1 standard for all units being evaluated.

To give you an idea of relative brightness, the following is an approximate brightness chart:

- 1 lumen: Roughly 10-times brighter than full moonlight.

- 10 lumens: The total amount of light given off by a candle (however, a candle's light is not focused like a flashlight). A small keychain flashlight emits about 5 – 10 lumens.

- 100 lumens: Approximate brightness of a big, old, 3xD-cell flashlight.

- 300 lumens: A good brightness for an all-purpose flashlight.

- 800 lumens: About the same as a 60-watt tungsten household lightbulb.

- 1000 lumens: Similar to a car headlight.

Power levels and modes

Many quality flashlights have several power levels. Some have "turbo" modes for temporary maximum brightness. Variable levels give you some control over the run-time.

Many lights have a "moonlight" setting that extends run-time up to several days, although you won't be able to see much using this setting. At a higher brightness level, your light may last for 30 to 40 hours. On the highest setting, the batteries may last only 1 to 2 hours.

Tactical flashlights

Very popular with law enforcement, these flashlights are designed to be tough, waterproof, and can be used as weapons. The heads are reinforced – some designed to break glass. They have strobe settings that can temporarily blind and disorient an attacker. Accessories include gun mounts and remote switches. While hikers and campers probably won't need all of these features, a tactical flashlight could come in handy if someone did attack you.

Battery types

The type and availability of replacement batteries may be a factor in selecting your new flashlight. Batteries come in various sizes and types – choose your flashlight with battery replacement in mind.

Throwaway

While most environmentally conscious people use rechargeable batteries, disposable types are still commonly used. The most common, readily available, throwaway batteries types are AAA or AA.

CR123 types are another common choice, but they are more expensive and can be difficult to find. The advantage of a CR123 type battery is higher voltage output in a smaller size, providing for bright, small flashlights.

With the arrival of better batteries and efficient LED bulbs, larger flashlights using C and D-cell batteries are losing popularity.

Rechargeable

Some flashlights use built-in lithium-ion batteries, and can be recharged in several ways. Some are equipped with USB charging ports, other models with charging stands. You can plug them into a household outlet, or use a charging port in your vehicle. Solar panels are another option.

Renewable

Less common, hand-cranked flashlights with built-in batteries are handy for emergency kits – some are even equipped with solar panels for recharging.

Cautionary note: To ensure damage does not occur due to mismatched battery types, don't use lithium or lithium-ion batteries with your flashlight unless recommended by the manufacturer.

Affordability

While shopping for a new flashlight, you'll likely be overwhelmed with the choices and price ranges. Flashlights range in price from less than $10 to more than $300.

Buying a superior quality light will give you a product that should last for many years. A good flashlight will give you the illumination you need with variable brightness levels making it possible to increase run time.

A high-quality light will be waterproof and shock resistant. If you need protection for walking at night, a tactical unit with a powerful strobe setting may be a good choice. You won't find these characteristics in a low-end flashlight.

If you're looking to buy a headlamp, most of the above factors pertaining to flashlights will apply. Hands-free headlamps are perfect for camping – cooking, gathering firewood, changing diapers, going to the bathroom, reading, pitching your tent, or just going for a walk.

A few additional considerations before buying a headlamp include:

- Weight and comfort: If you plan to wear the headlamp for long periods of time, buy a super-lightweight and comfortable model.

- Children's' models: Some headlamps are designed specifically for kids. They have lower intensity beams so they don't blind everyone, some have different coloured lights, and many turn off automatically after a certain time.

- Models for runners: Headlamps designed especially for runners have balanced light and battery placement, are totally waterproof, are lightweight, and have red tail lights.

Armed with all this info, you should be able to pick a new flashlight and/or headlamp that's perfect for your needs. We like to have both a headlamp and a flashlight for each of us, and sometimes walk around with both. Shine on!

Chapter 12: How to Choose a Tent

"It always rains on tents. Rainstorms will travel thousands of miles, against prevailing winds for the opportunity to rain on a tent." (Dave Barry)

One of the most important items on your camping list should be a good quality tent. It would be great if you could take a tent out for a test weekend before buying...but, since you can't, you have to make a decision another way.

Do you need a tent for the whole family? Are you a biker or backcountry hiker? Will you use it just a few times or hundreds of times? Do you want a tent with large windows and doors, with a rain cover that doesn't block the view? One room, separate rooms, one door or two? Do you need a weatherproof vestibule or "mud room" for outside storage?

Consider the following before buying your new tent.

Affordability

Before you begin your search for the perfect tent, decide on a price range to suit your budget. Buy the best tent you can afford.

Quality and durability

Do you want a tent that will last for years or one that you may have to throw out after just one trip? If you camp with children and dogs, you'll need a well-made, ruggedly constructed model. The poles, zippers, seams, and tie-down connections need to be strong. Your tent may be transformed into a play area with children and dogs bouncing off the walls.

Size, comfort, sleeping capacity

A tent always seems too small. To be comfortable, you may need more room than you think – you might even want separate bedroom areas. You will likely need storage space for clothing, supplies, toys, dog paraphernalia, etc.

Manufacturers usually specify the per-person size of their tents – consider buying one at least one person-size larger. It's nice to have lots of room, especially if you have children and/or pets.

You may need more than one door – midnight bathroom breaks, crawling over the rest of the family to get out, can be a nuisance.

Weight and packed size

Do you plan to do any backpacking, or are you strictly a car-camper? Do you have limited space in your vehicle? Do you intend to use walk-in sites, or do some wilderness camping? Consider this carefully – unless you plan to buy more than one tent for different purposes.

Weather-resistance

This one's obvious. You will encounter wind and rain at some point during your tenting days – make sure the tent you buy is designed to withstand the elements. If you plan to camp during the winter consider purchasing a 4-season tent, designed for high winds and snow.

Style

Do you want to be able to stand up while dressing, or are you okay with limited headspace? Larger dome and cabin tents are designed with spaciousness in mind. Dome tents are generally easy to set up and have sloping walls to resist wind. The slopes create less standing-up room inside. Cabin tents generally take longer to set up but are more spacious with almost vertical walls.

Ease of set-up

It's getting dark when you arrive at the campsite – and it's starting to rain. You're tired, the children are getting antsy. There are poles scattered all over the campsite – and you used the set-up instructions to start the campfire. You realize you forgot to charge your flashlight batteries as you experiment with dozens of possible pole connections. It rains harder. It might be a good idea to shop for a tent offering fast and easy set-up, with colour-coded poles!

Double or single wall

A single-wall tent has no fly/rain cover. The material is not very breathable, so condensation can be a problem. They are lighter, so are well suited for hikers.

Double-wall tents require a weather-resistant fly, installed after the tent has been erected. They are easier to ventilate through built-in windows with screens. The extra material and poles make this type of tent heavier and more suitable for car-camping.

Hammock camping

Hammock tents are becoming quite popular. Not for the whole family – unless each family member has their own hammock – swinging from the trees sounds like fun. You may need to learn how to tie a few knots.

Technical stuff

You may see number and letter ratings in the specs for some tents. What do they mean?

"D": Denier ratings represent the thickness of the tent fabric's fibres – the higher the number, the stronger and heavier the fabric.

"T" represents thread count. Along with the "D" rating, this determines the fabric strength.

"mmH2O": This is the waterproof rating, the higher the number, the more rain resistant. For comparison purposes, an average umbrella has an mmH20 rating of about 400.

Miscellaneous tent options

- Weatherproof entry/vestibule awnings for storing your camping equipment, muddy shoes, etc.

- Interior loops for hanging lanterns

- Interior storage compartments

- Consider buying a "footprint" to help keep the floor dry. Many companies offer footprints for their tents – alternatively, you could use a small tarp to place on the ground under the tent.

- Pockets for organizing books, flashlights, etc.

- Reinforced exterior rope guy loops for extra stability in windy conditions

- Freestanding tents can be moved without taking them down and don't require pegs for set-up – although pegs do give more stability.

- Tents requiring pegs for set-up are generally more stable in windy conditions.

- Space for sleeping pads, an air mattress, or an inflatable bed with room to get around is nice.

- Ventilation mesh is important for hot, humid nights – and being able to look at the stars with the fly off is a bonus – as long as it doesn't rain.

Tip: If buying your tent online, write down the measurements and outline the tent size on your floor with masking tape. Put your inflatable bed or sleeping bags inside – pretend you're camping. Do you have enough room? Take into consideration the sloping walls of dome-style tents.

Lastly, a few anecdotes and tent mishaps come to mind, which I feel a need to share with you.

While camping in the highlands of Cape Breton Island, Nova Scotia, we woke up in the middle of the night with a wet tent lying on our faces – heavy rain and strong winds outside. Needless to say, we were a bit wet – I think we slept in the car that night...

We stayed in Dinosaur Park, Alberta, during a long drought (actually, it was the very last day of the drought). Thinking it wouldn't rain – it hadn't for over a month – we decided not to put the fly on the tent so we could look at the stars before going to sleep. Big mistake – the stars were great, but we woke up through the night to a torrential downpour – drenched again. We threw everything into the trunk of our car and drove to an all-night diner where we spent some time with a group of happy farmers at three o'clock in the morning.

While hiking the West Coast Trail on Vancouver Island, British Columbia, we camped on the beaches. We woke up one night to the (very close) sound of the ocean – I guess we misjudged the high tide line.

We've pitched our tents on beaches, fields, rocks, and on top of a prairie dog nest after dark. We've had them blow down. We've had water dripping onto our faces through the night. We've awoken to find a small lake had formed inside the tent overnight.

But we've always had a good time. We've had a lot of laughs – usually after our mishaps, not during. Tenting is fun. It can be a challenge at times, but it's worth every minute. Go ahead – buy your new tent and commit to a lifetime of camping!

Chapter 13: How to Choose an Air Mattress, Sleeping Pad, or Bed

"I just got the best sleep of my life on this air mattress – said nobody, ever." (Author Unknown)

A good sleep is arguably the single most important aspect of camping. Buying a comfortable bed, whether it's an air mattress bed on a raised frame or a slab of comfy foam on the ground, should be high on your priority list.

Types of Mattresses, Cots, Pads, and Pumps

The many options for sleeping equipment can make your decision totally confusing. This chapter will help make your decision an educated one.

Self-Inflating Mattresses

The insides of these mattresses are filled with open cell foam. It expands and fills with air when you open the valve – magic! The foam also serves as insulation from the cold ground.

Self-inflating mats are softer than a traditional air mattress due to the foam construction. However, they are larger to stow and heavier. They also tend to be on the expensive side.

Air Bed Mattresses

This type of mattress needs to be inflated – either blowing it up manually or by using some type of pump (refer to the "Pumps" section below). Stand-alone mattresses are placed on the ground. Models with metal frames and types with an inflatable base will raise you up off the floor to a comfortable height.

Since pump-up beds are filled only with air, they tend to be a bit bouncy and don't provide any insulation value. Some can be used as rafts for summer fun – our kids had loads of fun on the water with theirs.

If you have lots of room in your vehicle and tent, these mattress types are great for couples, families, and there may be room left over for pets. Our dogs would never sleep on the ground!

Mattresses with Frames

Instead of sleeping a few inches up from the ground, you can choose to buy a mattress with a frame. If you already own a good mattress you can simply buy a suitable frame to fit the mattress.

A good frame for car camping will be fairly compact and easy to use. Most simply fold out easily and fit in a small bag. Some are inflatable.

It's much easier to get into and out of bed when you're up off the ground – just like at home.

Foam Pads

A conventional foam camping pad is very thin – about an inch thick – and isn't very comfortable. If you put it on an uneven surface with a few rocks, you'll feel the discomfort – all night long – especially if you sleep on your side.

If you decide to buy a foam pad, consider the thicker models for comfort. On the positive side, they won't puncture and they're easy to carry.

Some people simply visit the local hardware store and buy a big piece of closed-cell foam to place on the ground. Unroll it, throw it in your tent, you're finished! A chunk of foam six inches thick is comfy but takes up an enormous amount of room. They can also be difficult to dry out if they get wet.

Foldable Cots

Cots can be comfortable camping bed alternatives. It's easier to lie down and get up with a raised mattress than having it on the ground – and you can use single-sized models for outdoor seats. On the downside, they are kind of bulky and heavy.

Pads for Backpacking

Backpacking camping pads are designed to be compact, lightweight, and provide some degree of insulation from the ground when cold outside.

Pumps

Many camping mattresses come with built-in pumps, some are equipped with an electric pump, and others have an attached foot pump.

Electric models simply plug into the 12-volt power outlet on your vehicle. A pump with a higher CFM (cubic feet per minute) rating will inflate your mattress quickly, lower rated pumps can take a long time, especially with huge mattresses. Some are extremely noisy too!

Some mattresses are equipped with a foot pump mounted in the foot of the mattress.

Rechargeable and battery-operated pumps are available with some air mattresses. They can be separate units or built-in.

You can also use a hand pump – there are models available specially designed for air mattresses – or you can blow your mattress up manually (we've done this quite a few times).

What to Look for In a Camping Bed

One piece of camping gear you don't want to compromise on is a bed. You want to be comfortable –

period. We'll show you what to look for before you buy your new camping bed.

Comfort

Most high-quality mattresses are very comfy. Foam-filled, self-inflating pads are softer than air-filled models and may be more comfortable for some people.

Car-camping air mattresses put comfort 1st, backpacking pads are designed for portability.

If you sleep mainly on your back you should be OK with most styles. However, if you sleep predominantly on your side, a thin, 1-inch mattress may not be adequate – look into one that has a 2 to 3-inch thickness for added comfort.

Size and weight

Car-camping beds are big and heavy but most are super comfortable.

If you move around a lot – especially if there are two people involved – make sure you buy a mattress that is wide enough.

Backpacking beds are designed to pack up small and are usually inflatable in design.

One person? Two? Dogs and kids? You may need a queen-size bed – and a bigger tent!

Weight is a concern for backpacking – there are many lightweight sleeping pads available.

Types of Valves

Premium products come equipped with better, long-lasting valve assemblies.

Some models have two valves to make inflation and deflation faster.

Ease of use

Self-inflating models are made of open-cell foam. Most need a bit of extra air to firm them up.

Built-in pumps are super convenient, but require batteries. Many airbeds include a pump – some are battery operated, some rechargeable, and some can be plugged into the 12-volt accessory power outlet in your vehicle.

R-value

The ability to insulate you from the ground in cold weather is measured in R-value – the higher the number, the better the insulation value. If you plan to camp when it's cold, look for an R-value of at least 3, higher if you plan to camp in really cold weather.

Final Thoughts and Tips

- Forget your pump? Instead of blowing it up with your lungs, try this tactic. Take a garbage bag and fill it with air. Wrap the end around the valve opening on the air mattress. Squeeze the air out of the garbage bag into the mattress. Repeat.

- For air mattresses with 120-volt air pumps, you need a power source. A power inverter that plugs into a 12-volt accessory power outlet in your car will work.

- Before you buy a new camping bed, set up your tent. Next, lay out the measurements of the bed you're interested in buying with masking tape on the tent floor. Do you have enough room?

- Buy the toughest bed you can afford. There's nothing worse than waking up in the middle of the night to discover all the air has leaked out of your mattress and you're lying on rocks and holes. We've been there – several times.

- Make sure you have a good air mattress repair kit with your camping gear!

- A camping bed with a frame can double as a spare bed in your house or apartment when you have company.

- Some mattress models are pretty versatile and come apart – unzip the outer cover and take out the pad for backpacking trips!

- If you're tall, ensure you buy a pad or mattress that's long enough so your feet don't dangle over the end for the cat or dog to play with through the night.

- Air mattresses can be used for floating around on a lake – kids love it! Beware – the wind can blow a mattress away from the shore quickly.

Buy the best, most comfortable camping bed you can afford. Waking up repeatedly through the night, tossing and turning in your sleep, and feeling exhausted when it's time to get up in the morning can totally ruin your camping experience.

Chapter 14: How to Choose a Sleeping Bag

"Speaking of sleeping bags, has anything ever had a less creative name?" (Adam Carolla)

Good sleeping bags to keep you and the family nice and toasty-warm on your camping trips are a must. There's nothing worse than waking up in the middle of the night shivering – well, maybe waking up in the middle of the night soaking wet...

Types of Sleeping Bags

Before buying your new sleeping bag, you need to consider a few basics to help with your decision:

- Primary use: Will you be backpacking, car-camping, or maybe both? Do you need a sleeping bag for children, for just yourself, or do you need lots of room for you and your partner?

- Season: Do you need just a summer bag, or a really warm one for camping all year round?

- Cost: Are you willing to pay upwards of $400 or less than $100?

Car-camping Styles

Car-camping sleeping bags are not designed with size and weight in mind like backpacking models. They are made for comfort and some are bulky and quite heavy. They have more room, are more comfortable than backpacking bags, and are more economical.

Backpacking Models

Sleeping bags designed for backpacking are lightweight, warm, and pack up compactly. Typical mummy bags come with a hood to keep your head warm, and are tapered to reduce the amount of unused space needed to keep the rest of your body warm. Some people find them claustrophobic with little room to move your legs and feet.

Some models are labeled as "quilts" and are used like a blanket or quilt. They have a short zipper at the bottom to form a pocket for your feet. Quilts are placed on insulated sleeping pads and secured with ties – they don't zip all the way up like a sleeping bag. They are normally lighter and smaller than mummy-style bags with hoods.

Backpacking bags are usually made with top-quality materials, such as down filling, and can be pretty expensive.

Children's Sleeping Bags

You can buy smaller sleeping bags for children. Perhaps the most important aspect of buying one for kids is the size. If it's too big, it will be difficult for the body's generated heat to keep the extra space inside warm. On the other hand, you probably don't want to buy a new sleeping bag every year or two. Decisions, decisions…

One option is to buy one that's too big and cinch off the extra space at the bottom or fill it with clothing, stuffed animals, etc.

Wearable Sleeping Bags

A sleeping bag that you wear you say? Instead of putting on a jacket when you get up in the morning you can wear your sleeping bag. Hmmm… I'm picturing this and smiling. Anyhow, they are generally not as warm or as comfortable as a traditional sleeping bag. Some people claim to wear them while backpacking instead of a jacket to save space and weight.

What to Look for In a Sleeping Bag

Careful consideration of the following factors will help you buy a sleeping bag that suits your needs.

Warmth

The insulation used for sleeping bags is either polyester or natural goose or duck down. In general, the thicker the insulation material, the warmer the bag will be.

Down has a much higher warmth-to-weight ratio than polyester, so is the warmest for its weight.

A disadvantage with down is when it gets wet it loses its thickness and therefore its warmth.

Look at the down fill specs – the higher the number, the smaller the feathers. Small feathers are warmer, and they will dry faster than large feathers if you get your bag wet.

Temperature Ratings

Most sleeping bags list a manufacturer's temperature rating. You can use these numbers to compare products you are interested in buying.

Buying a sleeping bag that's rated for lower temperatures than you plan to encounter will ensure you stay warm.

If you plan to camp strictly during warm, summer nights don't overdo it and buy a bag that's rated for below-zero temperatures. You'll be way too warm and uncomfortable.

Size and Weight

Down is the preferred insulation for backpacking sleeping bags. Down-filled bags are lightweight, pack up small, last longer than synthetic, but are more expensive.

Synthetic insulation is bulkier and heavier, but is cheaper and is suitable for car-camping.

A synthetic-filled bag will be less expensive than down, will dry out quicker if you get it wet, and will insulate better when wet.

Features and Options

Adjustable girths make fitting the sleeping bag to your body possible, getting rid of unwanted cold air pockets.

Draft tubes, located along the zippers, help keep cold air out.

Draft collars, or neck baffles, keep cold air from entering your sleeping bag around your neck and shoulders.

Final Thoughts and Tips

- Down sleeping bags are more difficult to wash and re-fluff, synthetic you can just throw into the washer and dryer.

- Are you allergic to down?

- Sleeping bags filled with down will compress to about half the size and weigh up to 50% less than a comparable synthetic-filled bag.

- Make sure your body will fit the bag before buying. Most companies list girth sizes on their websites. You could possibly pin a sheet or blanket to the size specified and crawl inside to check it out. You don't want one too small or you'll be uncomfortable – one too big and your body will have a hard time keeping the extra space warm.

- Never lay your sleeping bag directly on the ground – always use some type of pad to retain your body heat. An uninsulated air mattress is a bad choice – the air in the mattress will be the same temperature as the outside air.

- The fluff (or loft) is compressed when you lie on your sleeping bag, significantly lowering the insulation value of the compressed sections. Always have something to place on the ground that provides some type of insulation, such as an insulated sleeping pad or a piece of foam.

- Eating before bedtime may cause your body temperature to drop while you sleep.

- Warm yourself up before getting into your sleeping bag on a cold night. Do some exercises, go for a run, whatever. Your body will warm the air in the bag much better and you'll stay warm longer.

- Keep the top of the sleeping bag cinched around your neck to keep the heat inside. Mummy-style bags are designed with this in mind.

- Don't go to bed wearing damp or wet clothing.

- Make absolutely sure your sleeping bag is 100% dry before storing it or it may become mouldy.

- Store it either hanging up or in a breathable bag. Do not compress it. It will maintain its "loft" (thickness) and last much longer.

- Down will retain its loft after repeated compressions longer than synthetic, so is a better long-term investment.

- If you're like me, you just can't resist pulling a protruding feather out of your sleeping bag or pillow. Resist the temptation if you can! It'll just make the hole bigger for the next feather. Pull it back into the bag from behind.

- We've always used two single sleeping bags and zipped them together to make one big one. Two bodies are warmer than one. Am I right?

- If you go for zipped-together method, consider buying two sleeping bags of different temperature ratings – you can switch which one you want on top depending on how cold it is outside.

Waking up feeling refreshed after a warm and comfortable sleep will make your camping trip that much more enjoyable. Buy a good sleeping bag – if you can't afford a super-warm model, pack an extra blanket or two for those cold nights.

Chapter 15: How to Choose a Camp Stove

"People who like to eat are always the best people."
(Julia Child)

We like to cook over an open fire, but for making a quick pot of coffee in the morning and cooking breakfast, we usually use our portable stove.

With so many stoves on the market, it can be a difficult to choose the right one.

Types of Camping Stoves

There are two basic types of camping stoves: large, heavier units for transporting in your car, and compact, lightweight models to take with you on backpacking trips.

Car-Camping Stoves

If you have lots of room and weight isn't a determining factor, a larger car-camping stove will give you a stable surface with lots of cooking space.

Models include tabletop designs and freestanding units with legs. You can choose a model with just one or multiple burners.

Many people prefer grilling. You can choose a stove with a built-in grill/griddle plate, or buy an add-on cast iron plate to fit over the burners on your stove. The add-on grill is, in my opinion, the best and most versatile option. The grill will cover both burners for a large grilling area, or can be removed for using two separate burners.

Some models have a grill on one side and a single burner on the other - we have one of these and find it very handy and versatile.

Backpacking Stoves

You really don't want to carry a three-burner, twenty-pound stove on your back on a long hike. There are super-compact units available that weigh next to nothing. Some are also very efficient so you don't need to carry a lot of extra fuel with you.

Small hiking burners lack the stability of a car-camping stove and they are made of lightweight materials, so can be a bit fragile.

What to Look for In a Camping Stove

A few factors come into play when shopping for a new camp stove. Consider each one carefully before making your purchase.

Do you want a stove primarily for car-camping? Do you plan to cook for just yourself, or a large family? Do you have lots or extra space to transport the stove and fuel? Maybe you need a tiny, lightweight model for backpacking.

Size

The size you need basically depends on the amount of food you need to cook. If it's just yourself, a single-burner table model will suffice – cooking for a large family may be easier with a 3-burner, stand-alone unit.

Single-burner units are adequate for couples who want to save space and weight. We prefer having a two burner stove – one burner for coffee, one for cooking breakfast.

A two-burner model should be adequate for up to four people – we made out just fine with our two-burner model with a family of four. You could buy an additional single-burner unit later if you find you need more cooking space.

Three-burner models mounted on legs will give you lots of cooking space, and you can put them wherever you want - not just on the picnic table.

Fuel

Fuel is also a deciding factor when choosing a camp stove. You can choose from gas, liquid, or solid-fuel stoves.

Propane gas stoves are simple to use and popular with car campers. Propane is readily available but can be costly. Small 1-pound tanks can be expensive, especially if you do a lot of cooking, and they cost way more than refillable tanks.

Buying a hose adapter to fit a larger, 20-pound tank will save you money, but they're large and heavy to transport. If you don't have room for a large, 20-pound tank, consider buying a smaller, refillable tank such as a 3 or 5-pound model.

White gas stoves are another option for car campers. White gas, sometimes referred to as naphtha, is a liquid fuel and is generally cheaper than propane. Some multi-fuel stoves can burn gasoline, diesel, or kerosene in addition to white gas.

Not as easy to use as propane and butane canister stoves, they come equipped with gas tanks that need filling – this can result in spillage – and the fuel tanks need to be pumped up to supply pressure to vapourize the liquid gas. They also require periodic maintenance such as cleaning and oiling.

Butane canister stoves work well for backpacking, and larger butane car camping stoves are available. The backpacking models are lightweight and compact, and produce ample heat for cooking.

Denatured alcohol stoves are compact and lightweight backpacking options. Fuel is relatively inexpensive, but does not produce as much heat as white gas, propane, and butane.

Solid-fuel tablet stoves are also used mainly for backpacking. They are usually slower to heat your food, but are super lightweight and compact.

Wood-burning stoves, another backpacking option, are small and lightweight. Some models can generate electricity to charge a mobile phone or other small device via a USB connection. You don't have to carry fuel with you – just collect twigs.

Final Thoughts and Tips

- Consider the size of the pots and pans you plan to use. Stoves with lids and side flaps can limit the size of pan you can use effectively. Open-topped models allow for almost any size pot – making it easier to cook corn-on–the-cob, clams, and lobsters!

- A possible arrangement to allow more than one person to cook at the same time is to have two stoves – a double and a single-burner.

- Freestanding models are great when you want the stove away from the picnic table or need more space on the table. They can be easily used with a large fuel tank placed underneath.

- Simmering capability is important - the flame is really difficult to adjust on some stoves. We had a stove where we had to turn it down ever so carefully - it went from full out to off in about a sixteenth of an inch space on the dial. It went out more often than not when trying to turn it down to simmer.

- Wind resistance is yet another factor to consider. You don't want a stove that blows out at the slightest hint of a breeze. It's not likely that you'll never encounter a windy day, so a model with windscreens might be a good option, rather than an open design.

- If you use a larger fuel tank with an adapter, and you have more than one stove to connect, you can buy a splitter to connect both stoves at the same time. Some models allow you to connect another stove directly.

- After you finish cooking your wonderful outdoor meal, be sure to turn off the propane at the tank (if using a larger, refillable tank) before shutting down the burners on the stove so there is no gas left in the line.

- Models with a piezo-electric start button make lighting easy.

- If you opt for a stand-alone stove, you might consider one with side tables for added convenience.

Whatever type of stove you buy, read the instructions carefully before lighting up. Pay special attention if you've chosen a liquid fuel stove that requires pumping and priming to ensure proper combustion and safety.

Due to the risk of **carbon monoxide poisoning**, do not use your stove in enclosed areas without adequate ventilation.

Conclusion

"Earth and sky, woods and fields, lakes and rivers, the mountain and the sea, are excellent schoolmasters, and teach of us more than we can ever learn from books." (John Lubbock)

This quote is so true. However, we trust you've enjoyed our book and it helps to make your next camping trip an enjoyable and memorable one.

We hope you enjoy the outdoors as much as we do, and encourage others to get outside – camping, hiking, canoeing…

You will have a few misadventures along the way. They are inevitable. They are always memorable. They should not prevent you from camping again. Have a good laugh. Don't take it too seriously – relax – enjoy the little things that make life special.

We've tried to include everything you need to know. If there is anything we've missed, please let us know so we can do revisions.

If you have any questions, suggestions for additional content, comments, criticism – anything at all – please email me at: zinckd@gmail.com

If you enjoyed this book and found it useful, please leave a rating and a review. Thank you!

Happy Camping!

39112507R00068